毎日の日本
英語で話す！
まるごとJAPAN

James M. Vardaman・山本史郎

朝日新聞出版

朗読音声について

本書の朗読音声))) は、
下記URLから自由にダウンロードできます。

検索方法
朝日新聞出版 🔍
↓
朝日新聞出版ホームページのトップページ右上の
検索欄に「毎日の日本」と入力してください
↓
「毎日の日本」のページから、
パソコンで音声データをダウンロードしてください

URL:
http://publications.asahi.com

＊音声ダウンロードは、パソコン回線で行ってください。
スマートフォンやMP3プレーヤーでご使用の場合は、
パソコンにダウンロードしたデータを転送してください。

編集協力	Karl Rosvold
録音協力	英語教育協議会
	東 健一
ナレーション	Howard Colefield 米
イラスト	齋藤太郎

毎日の日本

英語で話す! まるごとJAPAN

もくじ

本書の効用 ･･ 008

トレーニング・メニュー ･･･････････････････････････････････ 020

CHAPTER 1　日本のこころ ････････････････････････････････ 025

01	お茶　Tea ･･･	026
02	武士道　The Way of the Warrior ･･････････････････････	028
03	侘・寂　Wabi & Sabi ････････････････････････････････	030
04	いただきます・おじぎ　Itadakimasu & Bowing ･･･････････	032
05	遠慮・謙虚　Constraint & Modesty ･････････････････････	034
06	神道　Shinto ･･･････････････････････････････････････	036
07	祭り・御神輿　Festivals & Portable Shrines ････････････	038
08	仏教　Buddhism ･･･････････････････････････････････	040
09	お地蔵様 / 塔（仏塔）　Jizo / Pagodas ･･････････････････	042
10	お盆・お彼岸　Obon & Ohigan ･････････････････････････	044
11	禅宗　Zen (Buddhism) ･････････････････････････････	046
12	おもてなし　Japanese Hospitality ･････････････････････	048

CHAPTER 2　日本の食 ････････････････････････････････････ 051

13	出汁（だし）　Japanese Broth ･････････････････････････	052
14	日本酒　Saké ･･････････････････････････････････････	054
15	米　Rice ･･	056

16	寿司	Sushi	058
17	蕎麦	Buckwheat Noodles	060
18	醤油と味噌	Soy Sauce & Bean Paste	062
19	豆腐	Soybean Curd	064
20	海苔 / 漬物	Nori / Japanese Pickles	066
21	会席料理 / 和菓子		
	Elegant Japanese Dining / Japanese Confections		068
22	おせち料理	New Year Cuisine	070
23	ラーメン	Ramen	072
24	カレーライス	Curry Rice	074
25	和牛 / 佃煮	Japanese Beef / Tsukudani	076
26	包丁 / 食品サンプル	Japanese Kitchen Knives / Plastic Food Samples	078
27	弁当	Boxed Lunch	080
28	うまみ	Umami	082

CHAPTER 3　日本の伝統文化　　085

29	歌舞伎	Kabuki	086
30	能・狂言	Noh & Kyogen	088
31	文楽・盆栽	Bunraku & Bonsai	090
32	幽霊・鬼・妖怪	Ghosts, Demons & Goblins	092
33	浮世絵	Ukiyo-e	094
34	日本刀(刀)	Japanese Swords	096

CHAPTER 4　日本の文化　　099

35	侍	Samurai	100
36	忍者	Ninja	102
37	芸者	Geisha	104

38	日本語	Japanese Language	106
39	日本庭園	Japanese Gardens	108
40	国歌、国花、国鳥、国旗	National Anthem, Flower, Bird and Flag	110
41	旧暦	The Old Japanese Calendar	112
42	六曜・十二支	Rokuyo & The Twelve Animals of the Zodiac	114
43	金魚・錦鯉・鯉のぼり	Goldfish, Brocade Carp & Carp Streamers	116
44	相撲	Sumo	118
45	武道	Japanese Martial Arts	120
46	松竹梅 / 風呂敷	Pine, Bamboo and Plum / Wrapping Cloths	122
47	畳	Tatami Mats	124
48	七福神	Seven Deites of Good Fortune	126
49	温泉 / 招き猫	Hot Springs / Welcoming Cat	128
50	日本の四季	Japan's Four Seasons	130

CHAPTER 5　日本の社会　133

51	交通システム	Transportation System	134
52	交番 / コンビニ	Police Boxes / Convenience Stores	136
53	自動販売機	Vending Machines	138
54	居酒屋	Taverns	140
55	銭湯	Public Baths	142
56	天皇	The Empepor	144
57	判子	Official and Private Seals	146
58	やくざ	Gangsters	148
59	入学試験	Entrance Examinations	150
60	ヤンキー / カラオケ	Delinquents / Karaoke	152
61	アイドル / オタク	Idols / Otaku	154
62	お正月 / 駅伝	Japanese New Year / Long-distance Relay Race	156

CHAPTER 6　海外の方に人気の観光地ベスト10　159

63　伊勢神宮・出雲大社
　　　Ise Grand Shrine & Izumo Taisha Grand Shrine　160
64　日光東照宮　Nikko Toshogu　162
65　築地　Tsukiji market　164
66　浅草寺　Sensoji (Asakusa Kannon)　166
67　銀座　Ginza　168
68　東北　Tohoku (Northeast Honshu)　170
69　原宿・明治神宮　Harajuku & Meiji Shrine　172
70　富士山　Mt. Fuji　174
71　秋葉原　Akihabara　176
72　京都・奈良　Kyoto and Nara　178

本書の効用

ヴェネツィアと曼荼羅と
日本の学生

　私が7年ぶりにイタリアに渡ったのは、まだ東京の残暑が厳しい2014年の9月のことでした。前回同様、イタリア共和国の北東に位置する水の都ヴェネツィアにあるVenice International Universityで、世界中から集まった学生を相手に、年末までの4カ月間、日本についての講義をするためです。

　経済と文化の知見を修め、観光を学ぶこのインターナショナル大学は、アメリカのデューク大学、ボストン大学をはじめ、イタリア、イギリス、ポーランド、ロシア、ベルギー、ドイツ、オランダ、インドネシア、イスラエル、中国、日本など22カ国の計14大学が共同で運営するものです。日本からは私が籍を置く早稲田大学の学生を中心に20数名が参加しました。

　学生は全部で140人。文字通り世界のあらゆる国から学生が集まるなか、目立ったのは日本の学生でした。残念ながら良い面ではありません。コミュニケーションの方法と質において、一番子どもっぽく映ったのです。

　例えば、クラスで何かの発表をするときです。一番英語が不得手であるということに加え、日本人学生の話し方は平坦でメリハリがありません。イタリアをはじめ他国の学生はウィットに富んだ表現を用いますが、日本の学生はウィットを解することもできないことが多い。他国の学生は個々人の意見を堂々と伝えますが、日本の学生は助けを求めてキョロキョロする。イスラエルから来た、兵役を

終えた 28 歳の学生が大人なのは当然としても、同世代の他国の学生が備えている自立性と矜持に比して、日本の学生はやはり子どもっぽい印象を受けるのです。

　学生たちと、ヴェネツィア・ラグーン（ヴェネツィア潟）の中にあるトルッチェッロという小さな島に行ったときのことです。小さな教会を訪ね、内部の壮麗なモザイク画を鑑賞していると、イタリアの学生たちが、他国の学生に尋ねられるがまま、英語でモザイク画に描かれている登場人物の解説をはじめました。彼らは、決して地元のヴェネツィアっ子ではありません。日本に置き換えてみると、東京の大学生が、東北地方の古寺にまします仏像についての解説をしているようなものです。

　翻って、禅に興味を持っているイギリスの学生が「曼荼羅」を手に、日本の学生に解説を求めたとき、彼らは「仏を描いたものだ」と言うばかりで、それ以上の情報を伝えることができませんでした。おそらく、言うべき内容も持っていなければ、たとえ内容があったとしても、それを表現する英語コミュニケーション技術を備えていなかったのです。

　日本に暮らす者として、私は大変残念に思いました。おそらく、この日本の学生たちも、忸怩たる思いを抱いていたことでしょう。

　冒頭にこのような話をして申し訳ありませんでしたが、それくらい、日本の方々が、せっかく世界に誇るべき独自性と美点を備えた日本を紹介することが苦手だということをわかってほしかったのです。

　上記の例ばかりではなく、日本から海外への留学生が共通して言う言葉は「もっと日本のことを勉強してから行けばよかった」です。

　アメリカやイギリスの内容を扱った英語教科書が多かったせいもありましょうが、日本人の英語学習において、日本について英語で説明するための学習がおろそかになりすぎてはいないでしょうか

（私は、英語の先生こそ、日本にももっと精通しなければならないのではないかと思います）。

　人に何かを紹介（説明）しようと思ったら、たとえ母語であっても一定の準備をしなければなりません。まして、英語で日本を説明しようとする場合、トレーニングをしなければできるようにならないのはあたりまえです。

海外でのコミュニケーションでは、日本人は必ず日本のことを聞かれます。日本のことを紹介しなければならない場面が間違いなく訪れます。

　にもかかわらず、その練習をしている人はあまりいません。渡航先の国の文化を学ぶことも大切ですが、自国（日本）のことをきちんと説明できるようにする準備トレーニングこそ肝要なのです。

『風姿花伝』と大人のマナー

> 秘する花を知る事。秘すれば花なり、
> 秘せずば花なるべからず、となり。
> ——『風姿花伝』世阿弥　岩波書店より

　あまりに有名なこの一節は、600年ほど前の室町時代、能を大成した世阿弥が遺したものです。能の奥義を子孫に伝えるために著した『風姿花伝』には、芸能論、芸術論だけにとどまらない深みがあります。シェイクスピアが活躍する200年も前、大陸のはるか東方の孤島において、すでにこのような傑作が生まれていたことは誇るべきことでしょう（実際、海外の教室でこの古典を紹介すると、

一様に感嘆されます)。

冒頭の一節は現代語に言い換えると、

「秘することが花となることを知るべきだ。秘しているから花となるのであって、秘せずに明らかにしてしまうと花とはならない」

となります。つまり、「花は、内面に秘めているからこそ、いざというときに花として映えるのであって、常々晒すものではない」ということでしょう。日本では、よく女性の衣装を指して「秘するが花だよ」などと言われますが、これは間違った使い方です。「花」とは、普段は秘して見せない「花」であって、技や技能を指しています。

この「花」は、「あの役者には花がある」と同じ「花」です。巷間よく使われる「言わぬが花（言ってしまうと野暮になる）」という言葉も、同じ類の概念から生まれた言葉でしょうか。

このようなご説明は、読者の皆さまにとっては釈迦に説法でありましょうが、私は日本に来てしばらく、この「秘すれば花なり」の意味するところをきちんと理解することができませんでした。

私が「秘すれば花なり」という言葉を美徳と感じるようになったのは、日本人、日本社会の慣習や文化を理解するようになってからです。

来日当初は、『サザエさん』を読んでも何が面白いのかわかりませんでした。粋と人情とやせがまんの『男はつらいよ』の寅さんの良さがわかるようになったのもずっと後のことです。当然のことながら、私が生まれたアメリカには、日本社会に通底しているといってもいいような「秘すれば花なり」という共通概念はありません。日本のように海に囲まれた地形ではなく、陸続きの土地に異なる文化の様々な民族が暮らす欧米では、日本式の「言わぬが花。みなまで言うな」ではなく、むしろ**言わなければわからない。みなまで説明しろ**」という社会です。さらに、**教養を備えた大人ならば、も**

のごとに対して説明責任を果たすことは当然のマナーである、とされています。何かを聞かれたならば、それを自分の言葉で説明することが、大人の条件となるのです。

その点が、以心伝心のコミュニケーションを良しとする日本人の心性と相容れない部分であり、相互理解に齟齬が生じる場所になっているのかもしれません。

ですから、日本人が海外の方とコミュニケーションをとる際に、一面的には「秘すれば花なり」式の考えは忘れたほうがうまくいきます。たとえ日本国内においてであっても、海外のお客さんに日本人的な「以心伝心」「みなまで言うな」式のコミュニケーションを強いるのは無理なのです。そもそも前提通念が違うのですから。

日本全国、日本語という共通語を話し、地域の特色はあるものの、ほぼ同じ文化を共有してきた日本人にとっては気が付きにくいことですが、同一国民がほぼ同じ言語や文化を持っているということは、世界からみれば稀有なことです。

つまり、**海外の方と接する際には、日本人の自分にとってあたりまえで、「言うだけ野暮」と思えることでも、自分の言葉を尽くして説明することが必要**なのです。

「禅」について
１分間話せますか？

いざ、日本の事柄を言葉で説明してみると、それまで気が付かなかった意外な気づきを得ることもよくあります。

「日本の朝食はどういうものですか？」

「禅と仏教の違いはありますか？」

「芸者ってどんな人ですか？」

……

　例えば、朝食の質問にたいして「日本人の朝食には、和食もパン食もあり、朝食をとらない若者も多く、典型的な和食は、「ごはんと味噌汁と焼き魚お新香、それに海苔や納豆、卵を添えたものです」と答えるとします。

　すると、「味噌汁ってなんですか？　お新香ってなんですか？」という質問を受けるかもしれません。

　それには「味噌汁は Japanese soup です。お新香は Japanese pickles です」となんとか返答。そこまではいいかもしれませんが、さらに「素材、調理法、調味料、味は？」と聞かれて、英語で説明できるでしょうか。「鰹節と昆布の出汁のとりかたは……」「糠床の説明はなんとすればいいのか……」、もしかしたら日本語でも答えられないかもしれません。

　「禅と仏教」の質問にいたっては、「禅は仏教のなかのひとつです」というように漠と答えることが関の山の人も少なくないかもしれません。おそらく、日本語で話しても、1分間以上語れない方もいらっしゃるでしょう。「芸者」についても然りです。

　知っているようで知らなかった自国の文化。わかっているつもりなのに言語化できない事象……。いかに自分が日本のあれこれをぼんやりとしかわかっていなかったか気付く人もいるのではないでしょうか。

阿吽の呼吸と
"agree to disagree"

　一方、特に海外の方とのコミュニケーションにおいて、自分の考えを表明することも大切です。

欧米に行った日本人留学生には、授業でどんどん発言する欧米の学生を見て、「初めは萎縮したけれど、よくよく聞いてみると、彼ら（他国の学生）はあたりまえの凡庸な意見しか言っていない。そんなわかりきったことを言って何になるのか？　意味があるのか？」という学生もいました。

　あたりまえの意見の表明であっても、もちろん意味のあることです。**「自分が賛成なのか、反対なのか、どちらでもなく第3の立場なのか」、自分の胸の内を相手に示すことで、相手は安心して議論を進めることができるようになります。**たとえ意見が違う場合でも、"agree to disagree"、つまり「意見が異なっていることを認める」必要があります。

　これは、同時通訳の神様と言われ、昨年末に身罷られた國広正雄先生が、ことあるたびに若者に伝えていたことでもあります。「何も言わないでははじまらない。agree to disagree だ。間違っていてもいいから自分の意見をぶつけろ。話してみないことにはなにも分からない。ただし、自分の言葉（考え）で話すんだ」と。

　日本を代表するデザイナーの一人である佐藤可士和さんの『佐藤可士和の打ち合わせ』というご著書に、いみじくも、そのことを痛烈に捉えた記述がありましたので、引用させていただきます。

　　厳しい言い方ですが、しゃべらないのであれば、打ち合わせに参加するべきではないとすら僕は思っています。発言しないなら、出てこないほうがいい。
　　というのも、黙っている人は、本人にその気がなかったとしても、打ち合わせの場に「負のオーラ」を漂わせてしまうのです。いわば「黙るというパワー」が出てしまっている。…（略）…しゃべらないことによって、活性化しようとする空気を重くしてしまう。
　　——『佐藤可士和の打ち合わせ』佐藤可士和 ダイヤモンド社より

思い当たる方はいらっしゃいませんか。

　これはビジネス場面を念頭に置いていますが、基本的に海外では、どの場面にも同じような共通認識があるといっても言いすぎではありません。もちろん、実際にはそこまで極端な話ではないかもしれませんが、日本人にとっては、それくらいの意識でいたほうがうまくいくのではないでしょうか。国の異なる者同士、異文化間でのコミュニケーションでは、日本人があたりまえにあると思っている社会のコモンセンスも、ましてやその先にある「阿吽の呼吸」や「以心伝心」といった共通感覚も存在しないのです。

　前置きが長くなってしまいましたが、本書は、「日本のことを、どんどん英語で話せるようになろう」というコンセプトのものです。使える英語習得を目的とする「毎日の英語シリーズ」の中でも、とりわけ私が刊行したかったものです。

　海外の方々とコミュニケーションする際に、優れた日本の特徴の数々をうまく説明できない日本人を見るにつけ、ずっともどかしく思ってきました。日本に住んで40年、勉強を重ねてきたつもりですが、本書のテキストは日本についての説明です。アメリカに生まれた私の説明には拙い部分もあるでしょう。日本人の皆さんのほうが、深く知っている項目も多くあることと思います。異論がある部分や意に沿わない部分もあるかもしれませんが、英語表現のご参考までにとご高承いただけましたら幸甚です。

本書は、下記の3つを念頭に設計しました。

① **「日本人が海外でコミュニケーションするときの心構え」を明確にする。**

② **英文テキストを、日本のことを説明するための最低限の材料にしてもらう。**
　＊本書の内容は基礎の基礎です。「はじめの一歩」として活用してください。皆さんのほうがずっと深く、詳しくご説明できる項目もあるでしょう。ただ、どうやって英文にすればいいかわからない方も多いと思いますので、日本語に対応する英単語の選び方など、参考としてください)

③ **トレーニングを通じて、実際に日本について話せるようになる。**
　＊実際に英語を話せるようになるためのトレーニング・メニューをつけました。必ず目を通してからトレーニングに移ってください。

　本書でご紹介する私の考えは、40年間、日本人学生や海外の日本人留学生、外国人学生を教えてきた中で感じ、できる限り学生に伝えてきたものです。てらいのない王道ですので、物足りないと感じる方もいるかもれません。しかし、トレーニングすれば着実にできるようになります。英語の学習方法も、海外で実際に話せるようになるための方法も間違いのないものだと確信しています。

「秘すれば花なり」の
ほんとうの意味

　日本には、誇るべき文化が山とあります。むろん、私が好きになった世阿弥の『風姿花伝』もそのひとつです。

　前述しておいて恐縮ですが、世阿弥の言う「秘すれば花なり」とは、日本人が他国の方とコミュニケーションする際、ほんとうに忘れてしまうべきものなのでしょうか。
　たしかに、一面の意味においては忘れるべきでしょう。けれども、世阿弥が言う「秘すれば花なり」には、もうひとつの意味があるのではないでしょうか。
　冒頭の一節の続きを読んでみましょう。

> 秘する花を知る事。秘すれば花なり、秘せずば花なるべからず、となり。この分け目を知る事、肝要の花なり。そもそも、一切の事、諸道芸において、その家々に秘事と申すは、秘するによりて大用がある故なり。しかれば、秘事といふことを顕はせば、させる事にてもなきものなり。これを、させる事（にて）もなしと云ふ人は、未だ、秘事と云う事の大用を知らぬ故なり。
> ——『風姿花伝』世阿弥　岩波書店より

　現代語訳に直訳すると、
　秘めておくことが花となる、と知ること。この境界を知っておくことが肝要である。秘めておくから花となるのであり、秘めずに見せてしまっては花ではない。あらゆる芸ごとにおいて、その家々の

秘伝があり、それは、秘することで、いざというときに大きな仕事ができるから秘するのである。だから、秘伝を明かしてしまうと、たいしたものでもないものだ。しかし、これを「たいしたことがない」と言う人は、いまだ秘めておくことによって大きな効用となるのを知らないのである。

　この『風姿花伝』を著しているのは、当代きっての能の名人であり、申楽を芸術としての能楽に大成させた世阿弥です。能楽は、神経を指先や足の先はおろか、顔につけたお面の隅々にまで行きわたらせ、美しい所作で舞います。その優雅な歩き方、手の上げ下げひとつの裏には、信じられないほどの日々の鍛練の積み重ねがあるのです。
　「花」は明かしてしまうと「たいしたものではない」と言っておりますが、それは、世阿弥からみれば「たいしたことではない」ものであっても、日々稽古に励み、高度に洗練された芸です。
　それが、しかるべき場を得れば「花」となって舞うことができるのです。
　世阿弥は、秘することの重要性を説いた、その言葉の裏に秘した意味として、
　「いざという時に見せる花（なんでもないようでいて、洗練され、かつ新しい技）を磨いておきなさい」
　という意味を込めているのではないでしょうか。

　これを英語コミュニケーションに置き換えてみると、日々、普通の人は意識していないような日本のことがらを言語化できるようにし、かつ英語で紹介できるようにしておくことが、海外の方にとって「秘する花」になるのだと思います。
　世阿弥の『風姿花伝』はもともと芸能論であり、エンタテイメントの心得を著したものです。言い換えれば、日本人のホスピタリテ

ィの原点であります。

　おもてなしのこころ、おもてなしの技は、この原点に帰って備えることによって、ほんものを見せることができるのではないでしょうか。世阿弥には到底及ぶべくもなくとも、少しでも近づく努力をしなくてはなりません。

　筆者のテキストでは、深遠な世阿弥の境地を表すことはできませんが、まずは、はじめの一歩として、本書のテキストの内容を身に付けるところからトレーニングしてください。

　次頁に、具体的なトレーニングのメニューを記しました。ぜひ、お目通しください。

トレーニング・メニュー

Step 1 黙読する

　タイトルを確認してから、英文テキストを読んでください。わからない単語があっても、ざっと全体に目を通して、大意を捉えてください。

　次に、わからない部分と日本語訳を照らし合わせて意味を確認しましょう。色が変わっている部分は、キーワードや、覚えておくと使える英語表現です。日本語を英語で表現しようとするとき、どのような英語表現を用いればいいのか、そのご参考にしてください。

　どうしてもわからない表現がある場合は、辞書を使ったり、インターネットを使ったりして調べ、理解してください。

Step 2 目と耳で読む

　テキストの意味をすべて理解した上で、朗読音声を聴きながら、目でテキストを追ってください。

　朗読音声のスピードはナチュラルスピードです。その速さで聴きながら、同時に理解できるようになるまで聴きこんでください。

　耳で「発音・アクセント・英文の音の強弱・音のつながりと変化」を聴き取りながら、英語のリズムに合わせて黙読します。

　このトレーニングは、英語の速読力養成にも、リスニング力養成にも効果的です。ご自分で納得できるまで、何度でも繰り返してください。

Step 3 発話力を鍛える

　目と耳で十分にテキストを理解したら、口を使ってトレーニングしましょう。

　日本人に一番足りないのはこのトレーニングです。あたりまえのことですが、英会話は「会話」です。ご自分の口を使って英語を話さなければなりません。いくらテキストを完璧に理解しても、口を使って練習しなければ意味がありません。完璧なスイミング理論を理解しても、実際に泳いでみなければ泳げるようになりません。黙読だけで終わってしまっては、畳の上で水泳をしているようなものです。英語も、実際に口の筋肉を動かし、声帯を震わせて音声を発しなければ、決して話せるようにはなりません。

①シャドーイング

　朗読音声を追いかけるように口真似をしてテキストを読んでください。

　その際、テキストの意味をすべて理解しながら声に出しましょう。英文のリズムや抑揚まで真似することで、目、耳、口とあらゆる器官から、あごの筋肉の動かし方まで含めて、脳に正しい英語を刻み込むことができるようになります。

②音読

　何度も何度もシャドーイングを続けていくと、朗読音声よりも早く読むことができる方が出てくると思います。その段階か、朗読音声と同じスピードでシャドーイングができるようになったら、ご自分だけで音読をしてください。

　その際、なるべく朗読音声のようなリズムで音読することを心がけてください。

　音読を繰り返すことは、速読力・リスニング力・文法力・語彙力のすべての実力を底上げできるトレーニングです。だまされたと思って、何度でも繰り返してください。トレーニングは決して裏切りません。

Step 4 暗唱トレーニングで万全に

シャドーイングと音読を繰り返したら、暗唱に挑戦しましょう。
ご自分の好きな項目を選んで、テキストを見ずに暗唱します。

いきなり全文を暗唱するのは難しいので、まずは、1センテンスごとに暗唱してみましょう。1センテンスをサッと黙読したら、テキストから顔を上げて、暗唱します。1センテンスできるようになったら、2センテンス、3センテンス……とだんだん負荷を上げて挑戦してみましょう。
1項目、最後まで暗唱できるようになったら、今度は実際に海外の方に話しかけるようなつもりで行ってください。ジェスチャーも交えてスムーズにできるようになったら万全です。

Step 5 進歩の記録

トレーニングの記録をつけましょう。
語学のトレーニングは、1つのテキストを一回で終わりにしてしまっては非効率です。脳科学的な記憶の定着データを見ても、たとえば、同じ60分間学習するならば、1回でやるよりも2回×30分、それよりも4回×15分と日を分けて繰り返したほうが効果的です。
一回で終えるのではなく、2周、3周、4周と繰り返していきましょう。
また、2周目、3周目となってきたら、ぜひStep 4の暗唱トレーニングに挑戦してください。
トレーニングを終えたら、テキスト右上の記入欄に「月日」を記入してください。また、「シャドーイング◎」「暗唱トレーニング△」……など、ご自分でわかるメモを「月日」の上に記入してもいいでしょう。
その記録の積み重ねが、そのままトレーニングを重ねたご自分の自信の源になるはずです。少しずつでも歩みを止めなければ、必ず大きな成果を得られます。

三つの
初心不可忘

「初心忘るべからず」は、誰もが知っている言葉ですが、誰が遺した言葉が知っていますか。実は、これも世阿弥が『花鏡』という書のなかで書いたものです。そして、実は世阿弥の言った「初心」には、3つの「初心」がありました。

以下引用です。

> しかれば、当流に、万能一徳の一句あり。
> 　初心不可忘。
> この句、三箇条の口伝あり。
> 　是非初心不可忘。
> 　時々初心不可忘。
> 　老後初心不可忘。
> この三、よくよく口伝可為。
> ——『風姿花伝・花鏡』世阿弥　たちばな出版より

ほぼ現代語と同じなので意味は取りやすいと思います。「是非の初心」というのは、善悪の初心。つまり、わかりやすく正しいこと、よくないことを学ぶ初心者のころの初心です。

「時々の初心」というのは、人生の時々の初心ということです。みなさん、本書を手に取っていらっしゃる方々の中には、「やりなおし」と思って再度英語学習を始められている方も多いのではないでしょうか。一度は、英語を放り投げたとしても、再びモノにしようとされているその志、すばらしいと思います。

たとえ、「受験英語」で一花咲かせたことがある方でも、もう一度ほ

んとうに使える英語を身に付けようと思っていらっしゃる方もいるでしょう。

熟達の程度こそまちまちでしょうが、初心者でなくとも、その「時々の初心」も忘れないでください。

ご参考まで、「老後の初心」というのは、自分の身体が衰えたあと、その壁をどうやって超えるかという初心です。私は日本に来て剣道を学び二段まで取得しましたが、稽古で範士八段の先生を見て驚きました。ふだんは杖をついて歩かれているのに、いざ防具をつけて構えた途端、強い盛りの大学生の有名選手や 30 代の壮年剣士を手もなくひねってしまったのです。

皆さんも、本書にとどまらず、自分の言葉で精進を続ければ、いずれその境地に達する日もくるかもしれません。それまで、ご自分の花を大切に育んでいってください。日々のトレーニングは決して裏切りません。

James M Vardaman

Chapter 1
日本のこころ

01 お茶 [ocha]
Tea

Ocha usually means green tea brewed from whole leaves, but there is another type of tea, *matcha*, made from powdered leaves. It is found around the world. Ippodo, a three-century-old Kyoto tea seller, has opened a store in New York City. Starbucks and other cafés now offer drinks with *matcha*. You can find *matcha* ice cream, *matcha* mocha, and *matcha* soba noodles. The taste is popular and tea is known to include lots of vitamins and to be good for your health.

The ritual drinking of *matcha* is called *sado*, the tea ceremony. This ceremony came from Zen Buddhism, which was brought from China by the priest Eisai in the 12th century. Under Sen no Rikyu, the tea ceremony was perfected and became popular among the elite classes. In modern times, the tea ceremony has become a pastime for ordinary people. *Sado* is related to many other traditions, such as calligraphy, traditional poetry, and flower arrangement (*ikebana*).

Okakura Tenshin published *The Book of Tea* in English in 1906. In it, he explains how the world of tea represents certain important Japanese ideas. Tea is "an art of life" which embraces "vacancy" and around which there exists "a spirit that worships the imperfect." Through the philosophy of the tea ceremony, Tenshin attempted to outline the spiritual foundations of the Japanese people.

(220words)

「お茶」というとふつうは葉っぱを用いて淹れる緑茶ですが、もうひとつ別の種類のお茶があります。粉にした葉で淹れる「抹茶」です。どちらも世界中に広まっています。一保堂は3世紀続いている京都のお茶の老舗ですが、ニューヨーク市にも店を出しています。スターバックスなどのコーヒー店では、抹茶入りの飲料もメニューにあります。抹茶アイス、抹茶モカ、抹茶蕎麦というものもあります。抹茶の味は人気があり、お茶にはたくさんのビタミンが含まれ、健康に良いことが知られています。

抹茶を一定の作法にしたがって飲むのが茶道です。茶道は12世紀に僧栄西によって中国からもたらされた禅宗に由来します。千利休によって茶道は完成され、上流の人々の間に広まりました。茶道が一般の人のたしなみとなったのは、近年になってからです。茶道は書道、詩歌、生花など多くの古典芸能とも結びついています。

岡倉天心は1906年に『茶の本』を英語で出版しました。この本の中で、天心は、茶の世界には、いくつかの重要な日本の心が表現されていることを説明しました。茶とは「生の芸術」であり、そこには「無」が内包され、また「不完全なものを敬う心」が宿っているといいます。天心は、茶道の思想を通して、日本人の精神構造のあらましを説こうとしたのです。

02 武士道 [bushido]
The Way of the Warrior

  Bushi means "warrior" and *do* means "the way of." *Bushido* is a word that came into use in the Edo period. It was the ethical code of the samurai class, which ruled Japan during that period. "The Way of the Warrior" includes having the spirit of a warrior as well as skills with weapons. These were the skills they needed before the Edo period began. But once the Tokugawa clan gained control of the country, the role of the *bushi* or *samurai* changed. They were required to take political and intellectual leadership roles. They were required to show loyalty to their superiors, personal honor, devotion to duty, and courage under pressure. The samurai were supposed to devote themselves to service.

  Nitobe Inazo's book *Bushido: the Soul of Japan* (1899) introduced the ideas of *Bushido* to the West. The book described *Bushido* as an ethical system and a moral path. The chapters include key words such as rectitude, courage, benevolence, politeness, sincerity, honor, loyalty, and self-control. He believed that *Bushido* showed the moral character of the Japanese people as a whole.

(181words)

Round 1	Round 2	Round 3	Round 4	Round 5	Round 6
月　　日	月　　日	月　　日	月　　日	月　　日	月　　日

「武士」とは「戦う者」のことで、「道」は「〜の方法」という意味です。武士道という語は江戸時代から用いられるようになりました。この時期に日本を治めていた侍階級の倫理規範でした。武士道には、武術に加えて、侍の心を持つことも含まれます。武術は江戸時代が始まる前から必要とされていました。しかし、徳川家がこの国を支配するようになると、武士あるいは侍の役割が変わりました。政治的にも知的にも指導者の役割を果たすことが求められたのです。忠君、廉潔、忠勤、豪胆を示すことが求められました。侍は滅私奉公するものとされました。

　新渡戸稲造の『武士道 - 日本の心』（1899）は武士道の思想を西洋に紹介しました。新渡戸は、武士道とは倫理体系であり、道徳の指針であると述べています。「義」「勇」「仁」「礼」「誠」「名誉」「忠義」「克己」などをキーワードとして使いました。新渡戸は『武士道』という本によって、自分は、日本人が全体としてどんな倫理的性格をそなえた国民であるのかを明らかにしたのだと考えました。

03 侘・寂 [wabi/sabi]
Wabi & Sabi

file-03

Wabi is a taste for simplicity and quiet, free from worldly affairs. It emphasizes a simple, austere type of beauty. It encourages a serene frame of mind. *Wabi* is important in Japanese poetry, including *waka* and haiku. In the world of tea, *wabi cha* is a simple, austere, frugal type of tea ceremony.

Sabi is subdued refinement or an elegant simplicity. The word is often used together with *wabi*. *Sabi* includes loneliness, resignation and serenity. It suggests that although people may resign themselves to loneliness, there is a kind of beauty in that loneliness. Together *wabi* and *sabi* are central concepts in Japanese ideas of beauty in life and the refined arts.

It is said that the haiku of Matsuo Basho, who wrote *The Narrow Road to the Deep North* during the Edo period, include the essence of *wabi* and *sabi*.

Such stillness　　piercing the rock　　the cicada's voice

An old pond　　a frog jumps in　　the sound of water

(167words)

侘は世俗を離れて素朴と静寂を好む心です。淡白で素朴な美が強調されます。明鏡止水の心になりなさいと言われます。わびは和歌や俳句など日本の詩歌で重要です。茶の世界では「わび茶」というのが、茶道の中でも淡白で素朴で質素な流儀です。

寂は抑制のきいた洗練、もしくは素朴でエレガントな趣味です。この語はわびという語と一緒に用いられることが多いです。さびには、寂しさ、諦観、心の静寂などが含まれます。諦観を得て寂しい境涯に甘んじても、その寂しさこそが美しいのだというものです。わびとさびという２つの概念は、生活や洗練された芸術における日本人の美意識の中心を占めるものです。

江戸時代に『おくのほそ道』を著した俳人、松尾芭蕉の俳句には、わび・さびがよく詠まれていると言われます。

閑かさや　岩にしみ入る　蝉の声

古池や　蛙 飛び込む　水の音

04 いただきます・おじぎ
[*itadakimasu / ojigi*]
Itadakimasu & Bowing

Before beginning a meal, people in Japan say "*itadakimasu.*" There is no easy translation for this. It does not mean simply, "I am going to eat." It is an expression of appreciation for the meal. It shows appreciation to the host, the cook, and all of those who grew and prepared the ingredients. Many people were involved in making this one meal. Saying "*itadakimasu*" acknowledges one's indebtedness to them.

At the end of the meal, people say "*gochisosama.*" It is an expression of gratitude to the host or to whoever prepared the meal. In English, one might say, "thank you for the delicious meal." On one level, it is directed to one person. On another level, it is directed to all of the people who in some way made the meal possible.

· · · · ·

Bowing is Japan's traditional gesture of respect. It is used to show consideration for others during introductions, greetings and farewells. But bowing too deeply is as bad as not bowing deeply enough. An informal bow is about 15 degrees for people of all ranks. To make a formal bow, a person bends forward at an angle of about 30 degrees.

Bowing is also used with – or in place of – a spoken greeting, a request, an apology, or an expression of thanks.

(216words)

食事を始める前に、日本人は「いただきます」と言います。この言葉にかんたんに対応してくれる英語（翻訳語）はありません。これは単に「今から食べます」という意味ではありません。その食事に対する**感謝の表現**なのです。主人、料理をしてくれた人、材料を育て、準備してくれた人すべてに対する感謝の気持ちを表しています。この1度の食事をつくり上げるには多くの人が関わっています。「いただきます」と言うことで、そうした多くの人々のお陰を被っているという気持ちが述べられているのです。

　食事が終わると、「ごちそうさま」と言います。これは主人、ないしはその食事を用意してくれた人への**感謝の表現**なのです。英語では、「美味しい食事をありがとう」と言うかもしれません。これはある意味では、目の前の1人の人に向けられた言葉です。しかし、それとは別に、様々な形でその食事を可能にしてくれた人々に対して向けられているという側面もあります。

・・・・・

　おじぎは敬意を表すための日本古来のしぐさです。人の紹介、挨拶、別れなどの際、相手に対する気遣いを示すために行います。おじぎは深すぎるのも、曲げ足りないのもダメです。相手がどんなステータスの人でも、日常のおじぎは15度ほどです。あらたまった場なら、約30度の角度に頭を傾けます。

　口頭の挨拶、頼み事、謝罪、お礼の言葉などを言いながらおじぎをすることがあります。あるいは、そうした言葉のかわりにおじぎで済ませることがあります。

05 遠慮・謙虚 [enryo / kenkyo]
Constraint & Modesty

Enryo is an extremely important principle of personal conduct, and is translated as "reserve" or "constraint." It prevents people from imposing too much on others. In addition, it stops people from taking too much advantage of another person's kindness.

Out of reserve, a person may remain silent in a group of people. A person may keep his or her distance from others. Speaking without reserve or demanding too much of others are considered improper. However, exercising too much *enryo*, one cannot become close to others.

To make a guest feel comfortable, the host may say "*enryo wa irimasen.*" In response, the guest should keep a balance between accepting kindness and not taking advantage of the host's kindness.

Modesty is important in Japan. A modest or humble person keeps himself in the background. He doesn't show off. In a group, he may hesitate to speak, even if he has something worth communicating. He may hesitate to show a skill, even if he has ability worth showing.

Sometimes people take modesty too far. They lower themselves excessively. This forces the other person to encourage them to speak up or participate. This can be tiring for others.

This modesty originates from Japanese not wishing to go ahead of others, to be self-assertive, to stand out, or to show off one's abilities and in any way make others feel uncomfortable.

(226words)

Round 1	Round 2	Round 3	Round 4	Round 5	Round 6
月　　日	月　　日	月　　日	月　　日	月　　日	月　　日

　人としての振る舞いに、1つのきわめて大切な行動原則があります。英語に訳せば "reserve" もしくは "constraint" となります。すなわち「遠慮」のことですが、遠慮のある人は他人に対してでしゃばりません。遠慮深い人は、他人の心遣いに乗じすぎることがありません。

　遠慮のせいで、集団の中で沈黙してしまう場合があります。他人と距離をたもとうとすることもあります。遠慮なく喋ったり、他人に多くを要求しすぎるのは**無礼**とされているからです。しかしながら、遠慮がありすぎると他人と親しくなれません。

　お客にリラックスさせるために、主人が「遠慮はいりません」と言う場合があります。お客は心遣いを受け入れはするものの、それにずうずうしく乗りすぎることはなく、うまくそのあいだのバランスを取るのです。

　日本では、**慎み**は重要な美徳です。慎み深い人、すなわち**謙虚な人**は、いつも後ろに引いています。目立とうとしません。人中にいると、たとえ話す価値のあることを持っていても、話すのをためらいます。見るに価する見事な技術を持っていても、人に見せるのをためらいます。

　時として、慎みは行き過ぎることがあります。過度に卑下する人がいるのです。そうなると相手は、その人に対してなんとか話させよう、仲間に入れようと努力しなければならなくなります。周りの人はとても疲れる思いをします。

　日本人が謙虚になるのは、**他人に先んじて**でしゃばりたくない気持ち、目立ちたくない気持ちと、自分の力を誇示することで相手に不快な思いをさせたくない気持ちを持っているからです。

06 神道 [shinto]
Shinto

Shinto is the traditional religion of Japan. It developed from the ancient worship of natural phenomena, ancestors and *kami*. *Kami*, for which the closest English words are "gods" or "deities," are things or beings that produce emotions of awe or fear. A *kami* can be good or evil, but it always has mysterious power.

There are "myriads of deities," *yao-yorozu-no-kami*. Some are described in ancient Japanese myths. Others are the spirits of historical people and still others are connected with good harvests, prosperity, commerce and occupations. Farmers, fishermen, hunters and scholars each have their own protective deity.

Shinto shrines have a gate called a *torii* at the entrance. The main shrine hall, *honden*, houses the object of worship. This object is usually not visible.

Shrines often sell *omamori*, amulets, to protect against danger or bring good fortune. An *omamori* is a small cloth pouch which has an inscription inside. It is usually tied with a drawstring. This can be tied to a backpack or carried inside personal belongings. There are amulets for good health (*mubyo sokusai*), transportation safety (*kotsu anzen*), household safety (*kanai anzen*), success in business (*shobai hanjo*) and safe birth (*anzan*).

(193words)

Round 1	Round 2	Round 3	Round 4	Round 5	Round 6
月　　日	月　　日	月　　日	月　　日	月　　日	月　　日

　神道は**日本古来の宗教**です。自然現象や先祖や神を崇拝する古代の習俗から発達してきたものです。神は（英語にすれば gods、deities と複数になりますが）畏怖または恐怖の感情を呼び起こすモノ、及び生き物です。悪い神も善い神もありますが、必ず不思議な神通力を持っています。

　八百万(やおよろず)の神、すなわち「数百万の神々」がいます。日本古代の伝承から来ている神々もいます。でなければ、歴史上の人物の魂であったり、**豊作**、繁栄、商売、職業などと結びついている場合もあります。農民、漁師、猟師、学者にはそれぞれの**守り神**があります。

　神社には入り口のところに、鳥居と呼ばれる門があります。神社の中心である本殿には、ご神体（つまり崇拝の対象）が祀られています。それはふつう目に触れないようになっています。

　神社ではよくお守りを売っています。お守りというのは、護身除難、開運招福を願う護符です。小さな布製の袋で、中に詞(ことば)を記したものが入っています。ふつう紐を引っぱって口を閉じるようになっています。お守りはリュックサックに結んだり、いつも持ち歩く身の回りの品に入れたりしてもよいです。無病息災、交通安全、**家内安全**、商売繁盛、**安産**などのお守りがあります。

07 祭り・御神輿 [matsuri / omikoshi]
Festivals & Portable Shrines

Japanese festivals (*matsuri*) generally have their origins in the Shinto religion. They are related to the planting and harvesting of rice and to protecting the well-being of the local community. These festivals are held annually. They were originally rites to ask for help from the gods and to please the spirits of the dead. These days, some festivals have lost this religious nuance and are held to promote business and entertainment. Other annual events called *nenchu gyoji* come from Buddhist, Chinese or European origins. Together they form an annual calendar of interesting events.

Hina Matsuri, the Doll Festival, is a festival for girls held on March 3. Families set up tiered platforms for *hina* dolls (representing the ancient court with emperor, empress, and attendants). The Nebuta Festival, held August 2 to 7 in Aomori, features huge illuminated floats nine meters wide and five meters tall.

Omikoshi are often carried around during Japanese festivals. *Omikoshi* are usually called "portable shrines." The *kami* temporarily moves from the shrine to this portable shrine. It is carried on the shoulders of participants from the community. It may be carried through the local streets, onto a boat, or into the sea. Eventually, it is brought back to the permanent shrine and the *kami* returns to its original residence.

(215words)

Round 1	Round 2	Round 3	Round 4	Round 5	Round 6
月　　日	月　　日	月　　日	月　　日	月　　日	月　　日

　日本のお祭りは、たいてい神道に起源があります。田植えと稲刈り、地域社会の無事息災を守ることに関連しています。祭りは年に１度行われます。本来は神の力添えを祈願したり、死者の霊を慰撫するための儀式でしたが、今日ではこのような宗教的な意味合いを失い、ビジネス、見せものとして行われている祭りもあります。その他の年中行事には仏教由来のものも、中国やヨーロッパから入ってきたものもあります。それらが合わさって、興味深いイベントがめじろおしの１年のカレンダーとなっています。

　人形のお祭り、すなわちひな祭りは、３月３日に行われる女の子のためのお祭りです。各家庭で数列の段々を組み立てて雛人形を並べます（天皇、皇后、宮人などのいる昔の宮廷を表しています）。ねぶた祭りは８月の２日から７日にかけて青森で行われますが、横９メートル縦５メートルの巨大な灯籠が呼びものです。

　日本の祭りでは、よく御神輿が担がれます。御神輿は「動く神社」と言われます。神が一時的に、神社からこの「動く神社」に移ります。祭りに参加する地域の人々によって、肩にかついで運ばれます。かつがれて地元の通りを駆けめぐり、舟の上へと運ばれたり、海の中にまで入っていく場合もあります。最後は本来の神社へと運ばれてきて、神がもとの居所に戻ります。

08 仏教 [bukkyo]
Buddhism

Buddhism (*bukkyo*) was introduced to Japan in the 6th century, from China through Korea. Prince Shotoku is considered the founder and first great patron of Buddhism in Japan. He established several important monasteries, including the famous Horyuji temple.

In the beginning, Buddhism was promoted as the state religion. During the Heian period, the Tendai sect and Shingon sect were introduced. They were supported mainly by the ruling aristocrats and did not spread among the common people. During the Kamakura period, several things changed. Zen Buddhism was introduced from China. It was favored by the powerful military class in Kamakura. In addition, popular sects of Nichiren and Pure Land Buddhism began appealing to commoners.

Visitors from overseas may think that Japan is a Buddhist country. But that isn't really accurate. The Japanese themselves do not think they are religious or "belong to" a religion. Most Japanese today come into contact with Buddhism at New Year's when they pay visits to Buddhist temples. At *Ohigan* and *Obon*, they may visit the family graves, which may be next to the family temple. The temple and the priest who serve it are called on for funerals. Some temples operate kindergartens and offer Zen meditation sessions and even sutra-copying sessions.

(205words)

Round 1	Round 2	Round 3	Round 4	Round 5	Round 6
月　　日	月　　日	月　　日	月　　日	月　　日	月　　日

　仏教が日本にもたらされたのは6世紀のことです。中国から朝鮮を経由してきました。聖徳太子は日本における仏教の礎をきずいた人物で、仏教の最初の偉大な**擁護者**であると考えられています。有名な法隆寺をはじめ、いくつかの重要な学問寺を創建しました。

　仏教は当初、**国家宗教**に取りたてられました。平安時代には、天台宗と真言宗が入ってきました。これらを支えたのは主に**貴族の支配層**で、市井の人たちには広まりませんでした。鎌倉時代にいくつかの変化がおきました。禅宗が中国からもたらされ、力をもった鎌倉の**武士階級**の愛顧を受けました。それに加えて、日蓮宗、浄土宗など大衆受けする宗派に対して、一般の人々が魅力を感じ始めました。

　海外から訪れる人たちは、日本は仏教国だと思うかもしれませんが、これは正しいとは言えません。日本人自身、自分が宗教をもっているとか、ある宗教の「信者である」とは思ってはいません。今日、ほとんどの日本人にとって仏教に接するのは、元日に仏教寺院に初詣に行くときです。彼岸とお盆には、檀那寺の隣にある**先祖代々の墓**にお参りすることがあります。**葬式**のときには、お寺とそこの住職に面倒を見てもらいます。幼稚園を経営しているお寺や、座禅の会を催しているお寺や、写経のコースを設けているお寺まであります。

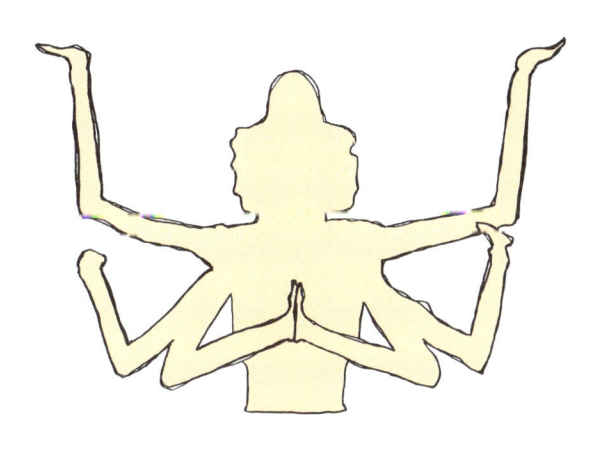

09 お地蔵様／塔(仏塔) [o-jizo-sama / to, butto]
Jizo / Pagodas

file-09

Jizo is a bodhisattva (*bosatsu*). A bodhisattva has not yet become a buddha, but already has the ability to become a buddha. Instead of becoming a buddha, Jizo pledged that he would stay in this world to help human beings. Jizo usually appears as a monk holding a jewel and a staff. He is considered the protector of children and travelers. He has been popular in Japan since the Heian period. The popular folktale *Kasa Jizo* about a kind-hearted old man is still told today.

· · · · ·

Pagodas (*butto*) are tall towers on Buddhist temple grounds for storing relics of the Buddha. The Japanese pagoda comes from the ancient Indian stupa. Some pagodas contain sutras or ritual implements instead of actual relics.

The Japanese pagoda usually has an odd number of stories. Many are five-story pagodas (*goju-no-to*). The roofs curve upward and get smaller toward the top. The structure of the pagodas was a model for the Tokyo Sky Tree — to withstand earthquakes.

(165words)

Round 1	Round 2	Round 3	Round 4	Round 5	Round 6
月　　日	月　　日	月　　日	月　　日	月　　日	月　　日

　地蔵は菩薩です。菩薩というのは、いまだ仏陀にはなっていないものの、すでに悟りを開いている［仏陀になる力を成就している］者のことです。地蔵は仏陀にはならないで、現世にとどまり、衆生を助ける誓いをたてました。地蔵はふつう如意宝珠［宝石］と錫杖［杖］をもった僧の姿をしています。子どもと旅人を守護するとされています。日本では平安時代から人々に知られるようになりました。心の温かいおじいさんを描いた「かさ地蔵」という昔話はとても人気で、語り継がれています。

・・・・・

　仏塔は仏教寺院の境内に建てられる高い塔で、仏舎利を蔵するためのものです。日本の仏塔は古代インドのストゥーパ［仏舎利塔］が伝播したものです。仏塔のなかには仏舎利そのものではなく、経文や仏具を収めているものもあります。

　日本の仏塔は層の数が奇数であるのがふつうです。多いのは五重の塔です。屋根は上向きにそっていて、上に行くほど小さくなっています。仏塔の建築様式は、耐震の面において東京スカイツリーのモデルになっています。

10 お盆・お彼岸 [obon / higan]
Obon & Ohigan

Obon is the Buddhist observance for honoring the spirits of ancestors. *Obon* was traditionally celebrated around the 13th to the 15th of July. But now that the Western calendar is used, *Obon* is celebrated in mid-August, instead. During this period, family members scattered around the country return to their hometown. Many companies give employees a few days off during this period. Trains, planes and highways are extremely crowded.

A spirit altar (*shoryodana*) is set up in front of the the Buddhist family altar (*butsudan*). This is to welcome the souls of the ancestors. The graves of the ancestors are cleaned. Horses or oxen made of straw or eggplant are provided for transporting the ancestors. A welcoming fire, *mukae-bi*, is lit on the 13th to show the spirits that they are expected. On the 16th, a send-off fire, *okuri-bi*, is lit so the spirits can find their way back again.

・ ・ ・ ・ ・

Ohigan is celebrated twice a year. Each is a weeklong celebration. One centers on the spring equinox and the other on the autumn equinox. During this time, Buddhist ceremonies are performed. These serve as occasions for paying respects at the family grave, in addition to *Obon* and the New Year.

(230words)

| Round 1 | Round 2 | Round 3 | Round 4 | Round 5 | Round 6 |
| 月　　日 | 月　　日 | 月　　日 | 月　　日 | 月　　日 | 月　　日 |

　お盆は**先祖の魂**をうやまう仏教の行事です。旧暦の7月13日から15日のあたりに行われていましたが、現在では西欧の暦が用いられているので、8月の半ばあたりに行われます。この期間の間に、全国に散らばっている家族が帰省します。多くの会社は、この期間の間に社員に数日間の休暇をあたえます。列車、飛行機、高速道路はとても混雑します。

　魂の祭壇(精霊棚)が、家の祭壇である仏壇の前に置かれます。これは先祖の霊を出迎えるためのものです。先祖代々の**墓**がきれいにされ、藁やナスでこしらえた馬や牛が、ご先祖様を乗せて運ぶために用意されます。13日には、霊が帰ってくるのを待っていることを知らせるため、迎え火、つまり歓迎の火がともされます。16日には、霊がもとの場所に戻っていく道が見えるよう、送り火、つまり見送りの火がともされます。

・・・・・

　彼岸は年に2度行われます。それぞれ1週間の行事です。1度目は春分の日を中心とし、2度目は秋分の日を中心とする1週間です。この時期には、**法事**が催されます。彼岸は、お盆と新年のお参りに加えて、先祖代々の墓にお参りする機会です。

11 禅宗 [zen]
Zen (Buddhism)

Zen is known around the world as the school of Buddhism that promotes the practice of meditation. The teachings of Zen were introduced from China and developed in the late 12th and early 13th centuries by Eisai and Dogen.

Zen had a powerful influence on ink painting (*sumi-e*), noh drama, tea ceremony, flower arrangement (*ikebana*) and the creation of Japanese gardens (*teien*). It was also important in religious writings and in secular prose and poetry.

The foremost Zen sects are the Soto sect and the Rinzai sect. The Soto sect is devoted exclusively to "sitting in meditation." The Rinzai sect is devoted to sitting and meditating on riddles (*koan*), such as "When two hands are put together they make a sound. What is the sound of one hand?" These practices are aimed at enlightenment (*satori*), a mystical experience that is beyond definition. They aim at thinking about absolutely nothing, putting the mind in a state of emptiness. This calms the body and the mind. Both body and mind enter an unagitated, tranquil state that is called samadhi, or meditative concentration.

(180words)

Round 1	Round 2	Round 3	Round 4	Round 5	Round 6
月　　日	月　　日	月　　日	月　　日	月　　日	月　　日

　禅宗は**瞑想**（座禅）の実践を勧める仏教の一派として、世界中に知られています。禅宗の教義は中国からもたらされ、12世紀後半から13世紀初頭にかけて栄西と道元によって深められました。

　禅は、墨絵、能、茶の湯、生花、日本庭園の誕生に大きな影響をあたえました。宗教書、世俗的な詩文のいずれにおいても重要な要素となっています。

　代表的な禅宗には曹洞宗と臨済宗があります。曹洞宗は「只管打座（ただひたすら座ること）」をもっぱらとし、臨済宗では「隻手の声（両手を打ち合わせると音がする。片手ではどんな音がしたか）」などといった「公案」について座禅を組みながら考えます。こうした行いの目的は**悟り**を開くことですが、悟りというのは一種の神秘的体験であり、**定義**するのは不可能です。参禅する者は全く何も考えず、心を無にすること目指します。それによって心身を静めるのです。そのような心身とも動揺がなく平らかな状態を「**禅定（三昧）**」といいます。

12 おもてなし [omotenashi]
Japanese Hospitality

Omotenashi is Japanese-style hospitality. It has the nuance of giving a warm reception and kind treatment to a guest. True hospitality means to anticipate the needs of a guest. The guest will rarely need to ask for any assistance, because it will be provided as soon as it becomes necessary.

In a traditional inn or in a private home, *omotenashi* tries to provide a peaceful environment and consideration for the guest.

The word was used in Tokyo's bid for the 2020 Olympic Games. Christel Takigawa, a representative for Japan, used the word in her speech before the International Olympic Committee (IOC). Her speech brought attention to *omotenashi* as a key word for Japanese kindness to guests.

(112words)

おもてなしは、日本流の**お客の歓待**です。この言葉には、お客を暖かく迎え、心のこもった対応をするというニュアンスが含まれています。真のもてなしとは、先々を読んでお客のニーズにこたえることです。お客のほうから何かを求めなければならないことはまずありません。必要に応じて、てきぱきと提供されるからです。

　伝統的な旅館や個人の家庭では、お客のために落ち着いた雰囲気とまごころを提供するのがおもてなしです。

　この言葉は、2020年のオリンピックに東京が名乗りを挙げた際にも用いられました。日本の代表である滝川クリステルが、国際オリンピック委員会（IOC）の面々を前にしてこの言葉を用いたのです。彼女のスピーチによって、日本人の客への心遣いを示すキーワード、「おもてなし」が注目されることとなりました。

このページに、使ってみたい英語表現や、覚えておきたい英単語などを書き込んでおきましょう

Chapter 2

日本の食

13 出汁（だし）[dashi]
Japanese Broth

Traditional Japanese cuisine (*washoku*) has become well known around the world. Two basic ingredients of *washoku* are *kombu* and *katsuobushi*. They are used to create *dashi*, a clear, subtle broth. This broth is the basis for miso soup and traditional dishes.

Kombu is dried kelp, found in food shops in short strips. *Katsuobushi* is bonito, or skipjack tuna, which is boiled, smoked and then dried. It is shaved by running the hardened dried fish over a plane. This makes extremely thin flakes.

Usually, both *kombu* and *katsuobushi* are used to create *dashi*. To make *dashi*, place a piece of *kombu* in a pot of water and put it on the stove. Just before it boils, remove the *kombu* and gently throw in the *katsuobushi*. Boil this for some time, then finally remove the flakes. A kind of umami flavor comes out into the broth, creating a mellow, rich taste.

Occasionally only *kombu* or only *katsuobushi* is used, and the resulting broth is called *kombu-dashi* or *katsuo-dashi* respectively.

In addition, families often have their own way of making *kombu-dashi*, *katsuo-dashi*, *ago-dashi*, *niboshi-dashi* and other types of broth. When a person tastes or smells that particular kind of *dashi*, it makes them nostalgic for their native place.

(205words)

Round 1	Round 2	Round 3	Round 4	Round 5	Round 6
月　　日	月　　日	月　　日	月　　日	月　　日	月　　日

　日本の伝統料理、和食は世界中で有名になりました。和食の2つの基本素材は昆布と鰹節です。この2つは、澄んでいて繊細な味わいの出汁（だし）スープをつくるのに使われます。このだしスープは、味噌汁や伝統料理を作るためのベースとなります。

　昆布は乾燥した**ケルプ（海藻）**で、食品店では短かく切って売っています。鰹節というのは、**鰹**を茹でてから燻製にし乾燥させたものです。かちかちに乾燥した鰹を**かんな刃**の上で往復させて削ると、ごくごく薄い削り片になります。

　通常、だしスープを作るには昆布とかつお節の両方を使います。昆布のひと切れを水に入れて、鍋を火にかけます。沸騰寸前に昆布を取り出して、かつお節をそっと入れてしばらく煮てから取り除きます。これによってある種の**うまみの風味**がだしスープに溶け出して、ふくよかでしっかりした味わいを生み出します。

　だしスープは、昆布だけで作られることもあれば、鰹節だけで作られることもあります。それぞれ昆布だし、鰹だしと呼ばれます。

　他にも、昆布だし、鰹だし、あごだし、にぼしだし……、と個々の家庭ならではのだしの採り方があり、日本人はそんなだしの香りをかいだり味わったりすることで、**ふるさとの郷愁を感じる**ことがあります。

14 日本酒 [*nihonshu*]
Saké

Saké is brewed from fermented rice. It is also called *nihonshu* (Japanese liquor) or *seishu* (pure liquor). It is made with steamed rice, yeast, *komekoji* and water. *Komekoji* is steamed rice fermented with *koji* yeast. Additional alcohol is added to some types of saké. These ingredients are mixed and fermented in several stages. The mixture may be allowed to mature for up to several months. Then, it is pressed, filtered, and bottled. Typical saké has an alcohol content of about 16%.

The highest quality saké is *daiginjoshu*. It is the top grade of *honjozo*, which is made from highly polished rice and has a mild flavor. *Junmaishu*, pure rice saké, has no added alcohol and tastes full-bodied.

Saké can be served warm in a saké decanter (*tokkuri*). You pour the warm saké (*atsukan*) from the *tokkuri* into small cups (*sakazuki*). Traditionally, people pour saké for one another. Nowadays, chilled *saké* is also popular with Japanese food and other cuisines.

It is said that saké dates all the way back to the Yayoi period. The current brewing method by saké-brewing artisans (*toji*) began in the Edo period. Recently the delicious taste of *nihonshu* is also enjoyed abroad and is called "saké."

(207words)

| Round 1 | Round 2 | Round 3 | Round 4 | Round 5 | Round 6 |
| 月　　日 | 月　　日 | 月　　日 | 月　　日 | 月　　日 | 月　　日 |

　酒は、発酵させた米から醸成されます。日本酒や清酒とも呼ばれています。それは、蒸米、**酵母**、米麹、水によってつくられます。米麹は、蒸米を**麹菌**で発酵させたものです。酒の種類によっては、追加のアルコールが加えられる場合もあります。これらの材料は混ぜられ、何段階かの発酵をさせられます。最大数カ月間、**熟成**させられることもあります。そして絞られ、ろ過され、瓶詰めにされます。普通の日本酒はアルコール度数が16%ほどです。

　最高級の日本酒は大吟醸酒です。高度に磨き込まれた米で作られ、柔らかい風味のある本醸造の最高級品です。**純米酒**はアルコールを追加しておらず、濃厚な味わいがあります。

　日本酒は、温められて、とっくりという日本酒用のデキャンタで供されることもあります。温められた日本酒、すなわち熱燗は、とっくりから、盃(さかずき)と呼ばれる小さな器に注がれます。お互いにお酒を注ぎ合うのが昔からの習慣です。今日では、日本食や他の料理と一緒に嗜む冷酒もまた人気です。

　日本酒の起源は遠く弥生時代にさかのぼるとされ、**日本酒造りの職人**である杜氏によって現在のような形で作られるようになったのは、江戸時代からです。近年、海外でも日本酒のおいしさが認められ、SAKE として親しまれています。

15 米 [*kome*]
Rice

In the Japanese diet, rice, not wheat or potatoes, is the main source of carbohydrates. Rice has less protein than wheat, but the protein quality is higher.

Rice is usually boiled and eaten plain. It is served in bento and meals at the table. Japanese rice is medium-grain rice, so the grains stick together, and it is easier to eat with chopsticks (*hashi*) than a fork or spoon. It can be formed into rice balls (*omusubi*). *Omusubi* can have salted salmon flakes or pickled plum in the middle. It is then wrapped with a strip of seaweed (*nori*).

Cooked glutinous rice can also be pounded into *mochi*. *Mochi* is a kind of rice dough that is eaten especially at New Year's. Rice is also made into a rice cracker called *sembei*.

Glutinous rice can be cooked with *azuki* beans to make red rice with beans (*sekihan*). This is usually served to celebrate life events.

Needless to say, rice is extremely important to the Japanese. Rosanjin Kitaoji, a Japanese artist known as a gourmet, wrote, "Rice is the most important part of a meal....A cook who does not know how to cook rice is not a first-class chef." (Quoted from *Okome no Hanashi*)

(203words)

日本人の**栄養摂取**では、小麦やじゃがいもではなく、米が主要な**炭水化物**源です。米は小麦よりも**タンパク質**の含有量は少ないけれど、タンパク質そのものはより良質です。

　米は、炊いてそのまま食べるのがふつうです。弁当でも、食卓での食事でも供されます。日本の米は中粒米なので、ご飯粒はねばっこく、フォークやスプーンより**箸**のほうが食べやすいです。ご飯はお米の団子、すなわち「**おむすび**」にすることもできます。おむすびは、塩じゃけや**梅干し**が入っていて、海藻で作った海苔で包まれます。

　炊いた**もち米**は、搗いて餅にすることもできます。餅は、お米で作った練り粉のようなもので、とくにお正月によく食べます。米は、煎餅と呼ばれるライスクラッカーにすることもできます。

　もち米は、あずきと混ぜて赤飯にすることもできます。これは、ふつう人生の節目などを祝うときに供されます。

　言うまでもなく、ご飯は、日本人にとって、とても大切なものです。食通で知られた日本の芸術家、北大路魯山人も、次のような言葉を残しています。「飯は料理のいちばん大切なものなのである。……飯の炊けない料理人は**一流の料理人**ではない」(『お米の話』より)

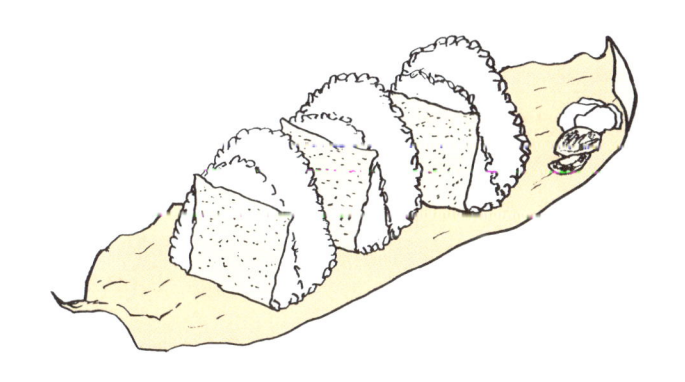

寿司 [sushi]
Sushi

Sushi is vinegared rice combined with ingredients such as raw fish, shellfish or cooked egg. There are four basic types of sushi.

Nigirizushi is made of a small handful of sushi rice with a bit of *wasabi* and a slice of raw fish on top. It is also called *Edomaezushi*. Instead of fish, it may have octopus (*tako*), shrimp (*ebi*), salmon roe (*ikura*), sea urchin (*uni*), or squid (*ika*). To eat it, dip it lightly in soy sauce. Eat it in one mouthful.

Makizushi, rolled sushi, is rolled into a cylinder. Common fillings include raw tuna and cucumber. The outside is a sheet of toasted nori.

Chirashizushi is sushi rice served in a bowl. It comes in two types. One has seafood, vegetables and sliced omelet on top of the vinegared rice. The other type has the vinegared rice and other ingredients all mixed together with shredded omelet on top.

Oshizushi, "pressed" sushi, is a specialty from the Kansai region. Marinated seafood and vinegared rice are pressed into a box-like wooden mold. Then it is cut into bite-sized pieces for serving.

In Japanese culture, a person who can skillfully eat and take pleasure in sushi made from ingredients in season is said to be a sophisticated, stylish person.

(216words)

寿司は、酢飯を、生の魚や貝、調理した卵などの素材と組み合わせたものです。寿司には、4つの基本形があります。

　にぎり寿司は、ほんの少しわさびのついた小さな一握りの酢飯に、生の魚の切り身をのせています。江戸前寿司とも呼ばれます。魚のかわりに、たこ、えび、いくら、うに、いかものせます。醤油に軽くつけ、ひと口で食べます。

　巻き寿司は、円柱の形に巻かれます。具は、まぐろやきゅうりなどです。酢飯のまわりは、1枚の炙った海苔を巻きます。

　ちらし寿司はお椀に酢飯が入っていますが、2種類あります。1つは、酢飯の上に、魚介類、野菜、薄い玉子焼きがのっているものです。もう1つは、酢飯と他の材料をすべて混ぜ合わせ、その上に細切りの玉子焼きをちらしたものです。

　押し寿司は、関西地方特有のものです。酢締めされた魚介類と酢飯が箱のような木製の型に押し込まれます。それを一口大に切り分け、供します。

　日本には、旬の食材を使った寿司を上手に食べて季節を味わうことのできる人を、「粋な人」だとする文化があります。

17 蕎麦 [soba]
Buckwheat Noodles

Many kinds of noodles are made from buckwheat flour. Usually some wheat flour is added. In *kakesoba* the noodles are served in a delicious broth with finely sliced long onions (*naganegi*) on top. In *zarusoba* the noodles are boiled and then served cold on a thin bamboo mat. The noodles are dipped into a dipping sauce with condiments like *naganegi* and *wasabi* paste. Like spaghetti, the noodles can be made just before cooking (*teuchisoba*) or dried and stored.

Buckwheat is nutritious because it has protein and vitamin B. The plant grows in cold mountain areas. These noodles are particularly good in prefectures like Nagano and Yamagata.

In Tokyo, the sophisticated way to enjoy noodles at a soba shop is to have something to eat and have a bit of saké before enjoying the soba itself. Good soba shops offer delicious side dishes including rolled Japanese-style omelette, slices of fish cake with *wasabi* (*itawasa*) and tempura. If one drinks saké, the graceful way is to stay within a limit of two and a half *go* (1 *go* = 180 ml) of saké.

(178words)

Round 1	Round 2	Round 3	Round 4	Round 5	Round 6
月　　日	月　　日	月　　日	月　　日	月　　日	月　　日

　そば粉から作られる麺にはたくさんの種類があります。ふつうは小麦粉が混ぜられます。かけ蕎麦は、**美味しいスープ**に入れ、上に細かく切った**長ねぎ**をのせて供されます。ざる蕎麦は、茹でられ、それから薄い竹の盛皿にのせられ、冷たい状態で供されます。この麺は、長ねぎや練りわさびなどの薬味を入れたつゆに浸けて食べます。スパゲティと同じように、調理する直前に作る場合（手打ちそば）も、乾燥させてたくわえられたものを調理する場合もあります。

　そば粉はたんぱく質やビタミンBを含んで、**栄養豊富**です。ソバという植物は寒冷な山地で育ちます。蕎麦は特に長野県や山形県のものが良質です。

　東京では、蕎麦屋で、蕎麦を食べる前に、肴といっぱいやるのが通の粋な食べ方とされています。いい蕎麦屋には、出汁巻き玉子、板わさ、天ぷら、といった美味しい肴もあります。酒は飲んでも「こなから（2合半）」までがきれいな飲み方とされています。

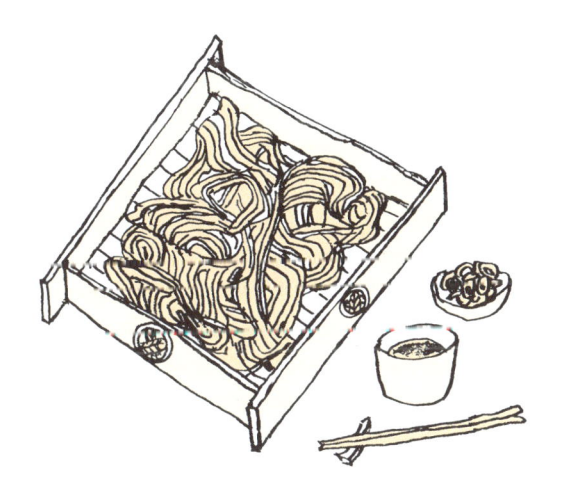

18 醤油・味噌 [shoyu / miso]
Soy Sauce & Bean Paste

Soy sauce and bean paste are two basic flavorings of Japanese cuisine. Both are made from soybeans.

Soy sauce (*shoyu*) is made by fermenting soybeans with water, salt, and yeast (*shoyu-koji*). Soy sauce is used in cooking and as a condiment when food is served.

Miso is made by mixing steamed, mashed soybeans with salt and yeast (*koji*), a fermenting agent. *Koji* is made by adding *kojikin* to different types of grains. *Kome miso* is made with rice *koji*. *Mugi miso* is made with barley. The mixture is aged in large wooden barrels.

Miso varies in color from a golden yellow to a dark brownish red. It also varies in saltiness, consistency and aroma. It is of course used in making miso soup. It is also used in cooking or marinating fish. Miso is also used in making pickled vegetables (*tsukemono*).

Miso originally came from China and was used as medicine among the nobility. In the Kamakura period, the custom of having "one soup and one dish" became common among the warrior class. As a result, miso soup became common. If asked to make a list of "good old home cooking," most Japanese would put miso soup at the top of the list.

(203words)

醤油と味噌は日本料理に欠かせない**２大調味料**です。どちらも大豆が原料です。

　醤油は大豆を水と塩と酵母（醤油麹）で**発酵させる**ことで作られます。醤油は料理の調味料としても、料理が出された際の味付けにも用いられます。

　味噌は蒸して潰した大豆に塩と、発酵させるための麹を混ぜて作られます。この麹は、それぞれ種類の異なる穀物に麹菌を作用させて作られます。米味噌には米麹、麦味噌には大麦を用います。混ぜあわせた素材は大きな**木の樽**で熟成されます。

　味噌の色は、明るい黄色から濃い赤茶色まで様々です。塩辛さ、粘り気、香りも様々です。味噌が味噌汁に用いられるのは当然のこととして、料理や、魚の味噌漬けを作るのにも用いられます。また、**漬物**を作るのにも用いられます。

　味噌は、もともと中国から伝わり、貴族の間で薬などとされていましたが、鎌倉時代に武士の食習慣として「一汁一菜」がひろまり、それによって味噌汁がひろまりました。日本人の「**おふくろの味**」といえば、その筆頭はお味噌汁です。

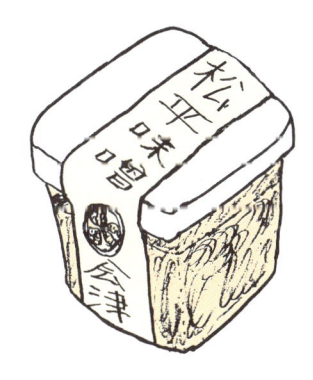

19 豆腐 [tofu]
Soybean Curd

Tofu is known around the world as "tofu." First, soy milk is made by soaking and grinding soybeans in water and then boiling and straining the juice. Then by adding *nigari*, it thickens into tofu. This is made in large blocks and sliced into small portions for sale. The main two types are *momendofu* and *kinugoshidofu*. The first type is standard. The second type is finer in texture and commonly used in summer dishes. Almost all varieties of tofu are delicious and nutritious.

Tofu is a common ingredient in miso soup. It is also served in *nabemono*, one-pot dishes cooked in a pot of broth. It is served warm in winter in the form of *yudofu*. In the summer, it is served cold as *hiyayakko*.

Tofu is said to have been introduced to Japan in the Nara period. In the beginning, tofu was a luxury food. In the Muromachi period, it came to be found in records of Kyoto temples and shrines.

In making good tofu, good clear water is essential. The reason why there are so many well-known *yudofu* and *yuba* shops in Kyoto today is probably because there are so many temples and because the city has an abundant supply of groundwater.

(198words)

Round 1	Round 2	Round 3	Round 4	Round 5	Round 6
月　　日	月　　日	月　　日	月　　日	月　　日	月　　日

「トウフ」は世界の共通語です。まず豆乳を作ります。大豆を水に浸けて細かく砕き、それを煮て濾します。ついで、ニガリを加えるとこの液体は凝固し豆腐の出来上がりです。出来たときは１つの大きな塊ですが、小さく切って販売されます。主要なものとしては木綿豆腐と絹ごし豆腐の２種類があります。木綿豆腐が標準です。絹ごし豆腐は肌理が細かく、よく夏の料理に用いられます。ほぼどんな種類の豆腐でも美味しくて栄養があります。

　豆腐は味噌汁の具によく使われます。鍋物（スープを満たした鍋で調理される、１つの鍋の料理）にも用いられます。冬には温かい湯豆腐にし、夏には冷たい冷奴にして供します。

　日本に豆腐が伝えられたのは奈良時代のことと言われています。はじめは高級食品であった豆腐が室町時代あたりから、京都の寺社の記録にたびたび登場するようになりました。

　また、よい豆腐をつくるのには、きれいな水が欠かせません。今でも京都に湯豆腐や湯葉の名店が多いのは、京都にはお寺が多いことと、豊富な地下水があるからでしょう。

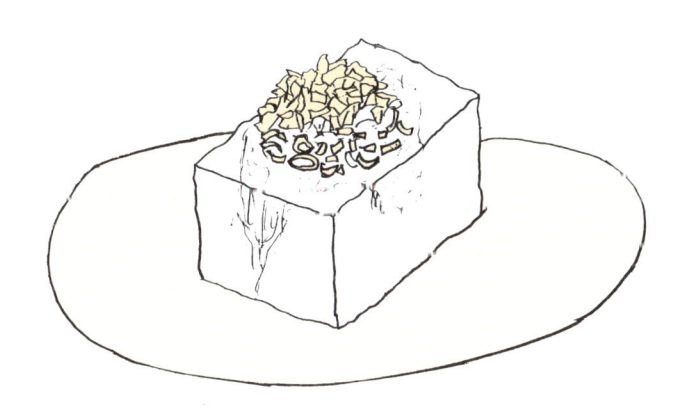

20 海苔／漬物 [nori / tsukemono]
Nori / Japanese Pickles

Nori is an edible seaweed. It is called "laver" in English. It grows naturally on exposed shores and is cultivated in some places. It is either purplish red or green, but both varieties turn black when dried. Dried *nori* is made into letter-size sheets and packed into bundles for sale.

Nori is toasted and used to wrap rice balls and roll sushi (*makizushi*). Nori is sometimes served with rice at breakfast. You use small strips of *nori* to wrap a bite of rice. It can also be wrapped around pieces of *mochi*.

・・・・・

Japanese pickles (*tsukemono*) are mostly made from vegetables. The base for pickles can be salt, rice bran (*nuka*), miso or vinegar. Turnip, eggplant, cucumber and daikon radish are commonly pickled vegetables. Lightly pickled radish (*asazuke*) is pickled in salt and ready to eat in just two or three hours. Pickled plums (*umeboshi*) take at least several weeks. *Takuan*, made from Japanese white radish (*daikon*), takes three to seven months.

Tsukemono is considered an essential part of a meal. In the past, each household made its own pickles, handing down special recipes from mother to daughter. Nowadays, although the tradition survives, people also like buying their pickles at the supermarket.

(202words)

Round 1	Round 2	Round 3	Round 4	Round 5	Round 6
月　　日	月　　日	月　　日	月　　日	月　　日	月　　日

　海苔は**食用の海藻**です。英語で言えば 'laver' です。海岸に自生していますが、それを養殖している場所もあります。色は紫がかった赤もしくは緑ですが、乾燥させると黒くなります。乾燥した海苔はレターサイズほどの長方形に整形され、それを束ねた形で売られます。

　海苔は炙って、おにぎりや寿司を包むのにも（すなわち巻き寿司）用いられます。海苔は朝食の際にご飯とともに出されることがあります。ご飯を海苔で一口ごとに巻きます。餅を海苔で巻くこともあります。

・・・・・

　日本の漬物は主として野菜です。漬けるベースとなるのは塩、**米ぬか**、味噌、酢などです。漬物によく用いられる野菜は**蕪、ナス、きゅうり、大根**です。浅漬というのは軽く漬けた大根のことで、塩で漬けて、ほんの2、3時間で食べられます。梅干しは梅の実を漬けたものですが、作るのに少なくとも数週間かかります。大根で作るタクアンは3〜7ヶ月かかります。

　漬物は食事になくてはならないものとされています。昔はどの**家庭**でも自家製の漬物を作り、独自のレシピが母から娘へと伝えられました。今日でもこの伝統は残ってはいますが、スーパーマーケットで漬物を買うこともよくあります。

21　会席料理／和菓子 [kaiseki ryori / wagashi]
Elegant Japanese Dining / Japanese Confections

Kaiseki ryori is a highly refined style of traditional Japanese cuisine. It is served in fine Japanese inns and restaurants. The full-course meal is served in several stages. Each comes on a separate dish, with great attention given to appearance.

There is a basic order. First there are appetizers, *sashimi* (sliced raw fish), *suimono* (clear soup), *yakimono* (grilled fish), *mushimono* (steamed food), *nimono* (simmered dishes) and some kind of *aemono* (cooked vegetables). Saké (*nihonshu*) may be served throughout this portion of the meal. The meal concludes with miso soup, *tsukemono* (Japanese-style pickles), and rice. At the very end there may be a Japanese sweet or some kind of fruit and green tea.

・・・・・

Wagashi are traditional Japanese confections. They have distinctive ingredients. The main ingredient is *an*, a sweet paste made of beans, sugar and water. No dairy products or vegetable oils are used. No artificial flavors are added. No natural flavors are used if they have a strong aroma.

Key characteristics of *wagashi* are their shapes, colors and names. Some *wagashi* are available throughout the year, but many are intended for a brief season only. They reflect the change of the seasons. For this reason, *wagashi* have long been a part of the formal tea ceremony.

(206words)

Round 1	Round 2	Round 3	Round 4	Round 5	Round 6
月　　日	月　　日	月　　日	月　　日	月　　日	月　　日

　会席料理は、上品なスタイルで供される伝統的な日本料理です。一流の旅館や料亭で出ます。フルコースだと次々と順番に料理が出されていきます。一品ごとに別々の皿で、姿の美しさにもたいへん気を使っています。

　基本的な順序があります。まず前菜が出て、刺し身、吸い物、焼き物、蒸し物、煮物、そして何かしら和え物と続きます。酒は最初からずっと出していてもかまいません。最後に味噌汁、漬物、ご飯が出ます。仕上げに、和菓子か水菓子（フルーツ）、それと緑茶が出るかもしれません。

. . . . .

　和菓子は日本の伝統的なお菓子です。和菓子独特の素材があります。主要な素材は餡です。すなわち豆、砂糖、水で作られる甘いペーストです。乳製品や植物油は使いません。人工的な香料も用いません。自然の香料も、香りの強いものは用いません。

　和菓子にとって重要な要素は姿形、色彩、そして名前です。1年を通して手に入る和菓子もありますが、短い季節限定品として作られるものも多いです。和菓子によって季節の移り変わりがわかります。和菓子が昔から茶道の一部となっているのは、そのためなのです。

22 おせち料理 [osechi ryori]
New Year Cuisine

Osechi ryori is special dishes prepared to celebrate the New Year. Originally it was prepared by New Year's Eve (*Omisoka*). Therefore, no one had to spend time cooking during the first three days of the New Year.

Each of the foods has some symbolic meaning. Some meanings are based on appearance and some are based on the sound of the word. Salted herring roe (*kazunoko*) represents prosperity and many children. Boiled and sweetened black soybeans (*kuromame*) are said to build a healthy body so that a person can work hard. *Mameni-hataraku* means "work hard." *Kurikinton* is a sweet confection made of chestnuts and sweet potato. Its bright yellow color symbolizes wealth.

Fish rolled in kelp (*kobumaki*) suggests *yorokobu*, meaning "happiness" or "being pleased." Steamed fish cake (*kamaboko*) colored red and white represents the rising sun of New Year's Day. Seabream (*tai*) suggests *omedetai*, meaning "congratulations."

Osechi ryori is time-consuming to make. Now many families order the items or buy them at a department store. Some families select only a few favorites and skip the others. Nonetheless, even now, the spirits of many Japanese brighten when they hear "*osechi*" mentioned.

(189words)

おせち料理は、新年のお祝いのために作られる特別の料理です。昔は、**大晦日**までに準備しました。そうすることで、**新年の三が日**の間、誰も料理をしないでもすんだ、というわけです。

　食材のそれぞれに意味が込められています。見かけに基づくものや、食材名の音にひっかけているものがあります。**数の子**（塩漬けのニシンの卵）は一家繁栄と子沢山を意味します。黒豆（黒大豆を甘く似たもの）を食べると、たくさん働ける達者な体になります。「まめに働く」というのは 'work hard' という意味なのです。栗きんとんは栗とさつまいもで作るお菓子です。金色なので富のシンボルです。

　昆布巻きは魚を昆布で巻いたものですが、「よろコブ」（という音）は、すなわち 'happiness'、'being pleased' を意味します。かまぼこは魚のすり身を蒸して赤と白に染めたものですが、**初日の出**を意味します。鯛は「おめでタイ」、すなわち 'Congratulations!' を連想させます。

　おせち料理を作るのは時間がかかります。現在では、デパートで注文したり買ったりする家も多いです。いくつか好きなものだけをピックアップして、あとは省略という家もあります。そうはいっても、今でも、「おせち」という響きを聞くと、心が華やぐ日本人は数多くいます。

23 ラーメン [ramen]
Ramen

Ramen is a Japanese version of Chinese-style wheat noodles. However, ramen is a Japanese meal, firmly rooted in Japanese culture. This highly popular Japanese noodle dish comes in many varieties. The broth can be made from chicken or pork stock, with kelp (*kombu*), bonito flakes (*katsuobushi*), a kind of mushroom (*shiitake*), onions, miso, soy sauce and salt. The noodles can be thin, thick, twisted or straight. A bowl of ramen may be served with a slice of fish cake (*kamaboko*), dried laver (*nori*), pickled bamboo shoot (*menma*) and a slice of roast pork on top.

For simple *shoyu*-flavor ramen, Tokyo ramen is well known. Kyushu is known for its *tonkotsu* ramen, which uses pork-bone broth. Hokkaido is known for its miso ramen. Many new types of ramen are being created to match different tastes in Japan and abroad. This evolution knows no end. Ramen cooks refer to ramen as "a full course meal in a bowl" and create ramen with great care and enthusiasm. Recently, dipping the noodles in a sauce before eating them has become popular.

(178words)

Round 1	Round 2	Round 3	Round 4	Round 5	Round 6
月　　日	月　　日	月　　日	月　　日	月　　日	月　　日

　ラーメンは中国流の小麦の麺類を和風にしたものです。ただし、ラーメンは完全に日本の文化に根付いた日本食です。このとても人気のある日本の麺類には、数多くの種類があります。スープはチキンかポークの煮汁に、昆布、かつお節、しいたけ、玉ねぎ、味噌、醤油、塩などを加えて作ります。麺には細いのや太いの、縮(ちぢ)れたのやまっすぐなのがあります。ラーメンを注文すれば、1片のかまぼこ、焼き海苔、メンマ（たけのこの漬物）をそえて、その上に焼き豚（叉焼）を1片のせたものが出てくるかもしれません。

　シンプルな醤油味のラーメンは、東京ラーメンが有名です。九州は豚骨ラーメンが有名です。豚骨ラーメンにはポークの骨のスープが用いられます。北海道は味噌ラーメンが有名です。日本や海外の様々な味覚に合わせて、新作のラーメンもどしどし作られています。その進化は止まることを知らず、「ラーメンは一杯のコース料理である」とも言われるほどで、ラーメン料理家はこだわりと熱意をもって新しいラーメンを生み出しています。最近は、ラーメンの麺をつけ汁につけて食べるつけ麺も人気です。

24 カレーライス [karee raisu]
Curry Rice

One of the most popular dishes in Japan is *kare raisu*. In English it is called "curry rice," "curry over rice" or "curry and rice." The curry sauce often contains vegetables like onions, carrots and potatoes. Beef, pork, chicken, scallops, shrimp or other seafood may also be added.

The British adopted curry from India. They then introduced it to Japan. Other types of curry from India and Nepal came later. "Curry rice" became popular in the 1960s, when resturants began serving it. Manufacturers also began producing the basic sauce, or roux, for cooking at home. Instant curry roux made a dish that is easier to prepare than other Japanese dishes.

Condiments that are served with curry rice include *fukujinzuke* and *rakkyo*. *Fukujinzuke* is a mixture of seven vegetables that are pickled with soy sauce, *mirin* and sugar. *Rakkyo* is a kind of scallion pickled in sweetened vinegar.

Today, curry is popular with everyone from children to adults, and it has become a popular item on the national menu especially among men. When it comes to curry powder consumption, Japan ranks second only to India.

(184words)

日本でもっとも人気のある料理の1つはカレーライスです。英語で言うなら、"curry rice"、"curry over rice"、"curry and rice" などとなります。カレーのルーには玉ねぎ、ニンジン、じゃがいもなどの野菜が入っていることが多いです。牛肉、豚肉、鶏肉、帆立貝、エビ、その他シーフードが加えられることもあります。

　イギリスはインドからカレーを取り入れてイギリス料理にしました。そのカレーをイギリスが日本に紹介しました。後になって、インドやネパールからその他の様々な種類のカレーが入ってきました。「カレーライス」が人気者になったのは1960年代のことです。レストランで出されるようになりました。また家庭で作れるように、各食品会社がタレのもと、つまりルウを生産しはじめました。インスタントのカレールウのおかげで、その他の日本のメニューより簡単に料理ができるようになりました。

　カレーライスと一緒に出される薬味には、福神漬け、ラッキョウなどがあります。福神漬けは7種類の野菜を、醤油、みりん、砂糖のタレに漬けたものです。ラッキョウは、ネギの一種を甘酢に漬けたものです。

　カレーは、今では子どもから大人まで、特に男性に大人気の国民的メニューで、日本のカレー粉の消費量は、世界でもインドについで第2位です。

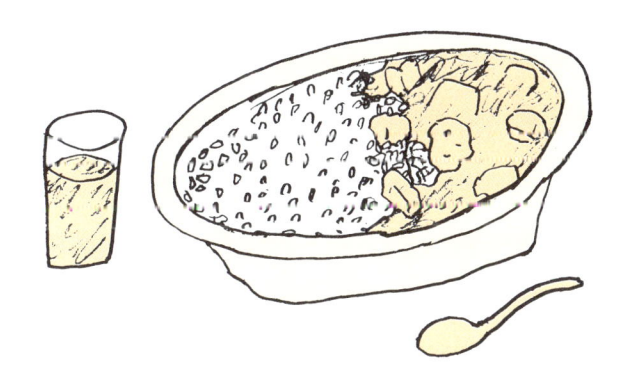

25 和牛／佃煮 [*wagyu / tsukudani*]
Japanese Beef / Tsukudani

Wagyu is a type of beef from specific breeds of cattle raised in Japan. Two of the *wagyu* breeds are Japanese Black (*kuroge*) and Japanese Brown (*akage*). These breeds produce beef that is highly marbled with fat. *Wagyu* beef is valued for use in *sukiyaki*, *shabushabu* and steak.

Wagyu beef is generally very expensive. In some countries outside Japan, the designation "wagyu" is used falsely just to raise the price.

・ ・ ・ ・ ・

On the other hand, *tsukudani* is a kind of food that spread among the common people of the Edo period because it was inexpensive and could be kept for a long time. *Tsukudani* is a type of preserved food. It is slowly simmered in a mixture of sugar, soy sauce and *mirin* until it is almost dry. The mixture gives it a sweet and salty taste. Preserved items include small fish, small clams, vegetables and seaweed such as kelp. *Tsukudani* is often eaten together with rice.

(162words)

和牛は日本で飼育される、日本独特の**牛の品種**から得られる肉です。和牛の品種には、黒毛、褐毛（あかげ）などがあります。これらの品種で**霜降り**肉が生産されます。和牛肉はすき焼き、しゃぶしゃぶ、ステーキに重宝されます。

　和牛肉は一般にとても高価です。日本以外の国では、値をつり上げるため「和牛」という偽のラベルが用いられることがあります。

・・・・・

　一方、佃煮は、価格の安さと日持ちの良さで、江戸庶民に広まった食べ物です。佃煮は**保存食**の一種です。砂糖、醤油、みりんのタレで、汁気がほとんどなくなるまでじっくりと煮つめたものです。タレによって甘くしょっぱい味となります。佃煮の具には、小魚、小さな**二枚貝**、野菜、および**昆布**などの海藻があります。佃煮はご飯と一緒に食べることが多いです。

26 包丁 / 食品サンプル [hocho / shokuhin sampuru]
Japanese Kitchen Knives / Plastic Food Samples file-26

Sharp *hocho*, high-quality Japanese kitchen knives, are the best in the world. Professional chefs value them for making clean, precise cuts. This is important in preparing vegetables, fish and meat, but especially in slicing *sashimi*.

Hocho are produced with the same care as Japanese swords (*katana*). They are forged and sharpened on one side of the blade only. This allows clean, precise cutting of soft ingredients such as fish, mushrooms, and tofu. The extremely sharp knives are essential tools for restaurant chefs and even amateurs appreciate their quality. Foreign visitors to Japan who are interested in cooking find a *hocho* a great item to take home.

・・・・・

There is a major industry that makes plastic replicas of food for display at restaurant entrances. These models of ice cream parfaits, tempura, bowls of ramen, and sushi attract customers to drop in. They are so lifelike that it is hard to believe they are artificial.

The best place to shop for these models is Kappabashi. This one-kilometer-long street is between the Asakusa and Ueno districts. Kappabashi used to attract mostly professional chefs. Today, however, it is also popular with amateur cooks and tourists.

(192words)

Round 1	Round 2	Round 3	Round 4	Round 5	Round 6
月　　日	月　　日	月　　日	月　　日	月　　日	月　　日

　鋭い包丁、すなわち日本の高品質の調理用ナイフは世界一です。きれいに正確に切れるので、プロの料理人にも重宝されています。この切れ味の良さは、野菜、魚、肉を調理する際にも重要ですが、特に刺し身を薄くそぐ場合に重要です。

　包丁は、日本刀と同じように丹念に製造されます。鍛えて研ぐのは片面のみです。それによって、魚、きのこ、豆腐など柔らかい素材もなめらかにきちんと切ることができるのです。鋭利に研ぎすまされた包丁はレストランのシェフになくてはならない道具であるばかりか、素人でもその良さがわかります。日本を訪れる外国人で料理に興味のある人にとって、包丁はおみやげの品として人気があります。

・・・・・

　レストランの入り口に飾る、プラスチック製の食品サンプルを作る一大産業があります。アイスクリームパフェ、天ぷら、ラーメン、寿司などのこうしたサンプル（模型）が、お客の目を引いて店に入ろうかという気にさせるのです。まるで本物そっくりなので、作り物だなんて言われてもまったく信じられません。

　このようなサンプルを手に入れるのに一番よいのは、かっぱ橋です。浅草界隈から上野界隈まで続く１キロの通りです。昔はかっぱ橋に行くのは、もっぱらプロの料理人でした。でも今では、普通の料理好きの人や観光客でもにぎわっています。

27 弁当 [bento]
Boxed Lunch

Bento are meals packaged in boxes that can be carried. These boxes include a complete meal, which may consist of rice, pickles, fish, meat, and vegetables. The boxes range from disposable plastic and Styrofoam to reusable wood and lacquer. Almost always, they have a divider inside that keeps the various dishes separate until eaten.

Bento may be prepared at home to take to school or to the office. Commercial bento are available at convenience stores. Bento sold at major railway stations (*ekiben*) are popular with travelers. These bento often feature a local ingredient or seasonal delicacy. One of the most famous types of bento is called *makunouchi bento*. It has rice, pickles and small bites of a dozen or so kinds of food. There are many legends about the name, and one of them says that it was created for eating between plays of a kabuki performance (*makunouchi*).

Bento bako, the actual boxes, are popular in Japan and abroad. Cute bento boxes may be colorful and have cartoon characters on them. Elegant lacquer boxes may have traditional Japanese designs or modern European designs. Bento-style meals, in which a person can enjoy many different dishes at one time, have become popular overseas, too. In France, some restaurants have become popular by serving *washoku bento* style.

(214words)

弁当というのは、携帯用のボックスにつめた食事のことです。ボックスには、ご飯、漬物、魚、肉、野菜などを組み合わせた、1回分の食事が丸々入れられます。ボックス自体はプラスチック製、発泡スチロール製の使い捨てのものから、**何度も使える**漆塗りの木製のものまで様々です。ふつうはまず、食べるまで中身が混ざらないようにしておく仕切りがついています。

　弁当は家で作って、学校や会社にもっていく場合があります。コンビニでは、弁当が買えます。大きな鉄道の駅で売っている弁当、つまり駅弁は、旅行者に人気です。駅弁には、地元の食材や**季節の味覚**を取り入れているものもあります。最も有名な弁当の種類は「幕の内弁当」といいます。幕の内弁当というのは、ご飯、漬物に10種類ほどの少量のおかずを添えている弁当のことです。この名の由来には諸説がありますが、一説に、歌舞伎の演目（だしもの）の間、つまり「幕の内」に食べるために考案されたからだと言われています。

　弁当箱（つまりボックスそのもの）は日本でも海外でも人気です。カラフルで漫画のキャラクターのついている、かわいい弁当箱もあります。上品な漆塗りの弁当箱には、日本の伝統模様や、現代ヨーロッパのデザインが描かれているものもあります。

　一度に数多くのおかずを楽しめる bento スタイルは海外でも人気です。フランスでは、bento スタイルの和食を提供するレストランが人気になっています。

28 うまみ [umami]
Umami

Umami is now considered one of the five primary tastes, together with salty, sour, sweet and bitter. Umami leaves a delicious sensation on the tongue and it brings all of the flavors of a dish together.

Dr. Kikunae Ikeda, a chemist at Tokyo Imperial University, suspected that there was a fifth taste. Ikeda did experiments to discover what created that taste. He found the taste in asparagus, cheese, tomatoes, meat and kelp seaweed. In 1908, he discovered that the delicious taste was created by glutamic acid. He named the taste "umami." This is the name that is used universally today.

Every food culture has ingredients that are rich in umami: Italians have it in mushrooms, tomatoes and Parmesan cheese; Chinese have it in Chinese leeks, cabbage and chicken soup; and Japanese have it in kelp seaweed, shiitake mushrooms, and dried bonito flakes (*katsuobushi*). Umami makes these ingredients taste better together than individually.

Delicate, eye-pleasing presentation of Japanese cuisine stimulates the "sixth sense" of flavor–beauty.

(171words)

「うまみ」は、現在では、「からい」、「すっぱい」、「あまい」、「にがい」とともに、5つある味覚の1つとされています。うまみは舌に美味しいという感覚を残し、料理の様々な風味をまとめあげる働きをします。

5つ目の味覚があるということに気がついたのは、東京帝国大学で化学を教えていた池田菊苗です。池田は様々な実験を行って、この味覚が何から生じているのか発見しました。この味が、アスパラガス、チーズ、トマト、肉、昆布に存在することを見つけました。そして1908年、この美味しい味がグルタミン酸によって生み出されていることを発見しました。この味を「うまみ」と名付け、それが今日広く一般に用いられているのです。

どこの食文化にも、うまみに富む食材が含まれています。イタリアでは、マッシュルーム、トマト、パルメザンチーズです。中国では、ニラ、キャベツ、鶏がらスープです。日本では、昆布、しいたけ、かつお節です。こうした食材をそれぞれ食べるより、合わせた味をよくしてくれるのがうまみです。

繊細な美しさで目を楽しませてくれる日本料理は、「美しい」という6番目の味覚も刺激してくれます。

このページに、使ってみたい英語表現や、覚えておきたい英単語などを書き込んでおきましょう

Chapter 3
日本の伝統文化

29 歌舞伎 [kabuki]
Kabuki

The three classical theater traditions of Japan are noh, bunraku and kabuki. Kabuki began in the early 17th century and was performed by troupes of travelling entertainers. In the early troupes, the women performers were very popular. They performed light theater with dances and comic sketches. Because the female entertainers also practiced prostitution, the Tokugawa shogunate banned women from appearing. As a result, all of the roles came to be played by men, including the women's roles. Actors who play these roles were called *oyama*.

Around the turn of the 18th century, kabuki had a major development with the appearance of professional writers such as Chikamatsu Monzaemon. The period also gave birth to innovative actors such as Ichikawa Danjuro and Sakata Tojuro. The new kabuki plays used the contemporary spoken language but developed a highly formalized style of acting.

The kabuki stage has an elevated runway from the main stage to the back of the theater called the *hanamichi*. It also has trapdoors and a revolving stage for quick set changes.

Kabuki actors wear brilliant costumes and spectacular *kumadori* makeup. On stage they use exaggerated gestures. They emphasize especially dramatic moments by striking dynamic poses called *mie*. Even a first-time spectator can fully enjoy a kabuki play. (216 words)

日本の伝統的な**古典演劇**は３つあります。能、文楽、歌舞伎がそれです。歌舞伎は 17 世紀のはじめに誕生し、旅芸人の集団によって演じられました。初期の芸能集団では、女性の役者が大きな人気を博しました。彼女たちが演じたのは、踊りや滑稽な寸劇を内容とする軽い演劇でした。女性の役者は売春も行ったので、徳川幕府は女性が舞台に出ることを禁じました。そのため、女性の役を含めてすべての役が男によって演じられるようになりました。女性の役をする役者は「おやま」と呼ばれました。

　時代が 18 世紀に変わるころ、近松門左衛門などプロの脚本家の登場で、歌舞伎は大きな躍進をとげました。また、この時代は市川團十郎や坂田藤十郎といった**革新的な役者**を生んだことでも注目されます。新しい歌舞伎では当時の**しゃべり言葉**が用いられましたが、高度に様式化された演技の型が発達していきました。

　歌舞伎の舞台には花道と呼ばれる、客席からせり上がった道があり、小屋のうしろまで続いています。また、床の上げ戸やすばやくセットを転換するための**廻り舞台**もあります。

　歌舞伎役者はまばゆい衣装を身につけ、「くまどり」という派手派手しいメークをします。舞台では、役者は大げさな身振りをします。特にドラマチックな瞬間を際立たせるため、「みえ」と呼ばれるダイナミックなポーズをとります。初めて観劇する人でも、歌舞伎を十分に堪能できるでしょう。

能・狂言 [noh/kyogen]
Noh & Kyogen

Noh is the oldest existing professional theater in Japan. It is an elegant musical dance-drama which began in the 14th century. Performances seem like a ritual and show a mysterious and profound Buddhist view of human life. The actors serve as intermediaries between the worlds of gods and men, so the plays do not deal with contemporary life. Movements are deliberate and highly formal. The actors, all male, usually wear masks, handed down within their troupes for generations. The performers are supported by a chorus, drums and a flute. A typical program today has two or three noh plays with half-hour kyogen plays between them.

Fushikaden, *"Transmission of Style and the Flower,"* written by Zeami, who perfected noh in the Muromachi period, has a depth not limited to noh as a performing art. *Fushikaden* contains a passage that almost every Japanese knows: "If it is hidden, it is the Flower."

Kyogen is a kind of comic drama that is performed between noh plays. It is the opposite of the solemn noh in every respect. It draws on the real world for its material. The characters have weaknesses, compassion, and humor. As a result, it has more mass appeal.

(203words)

| Round 1 | Round 2 | Round 3 | Round 4 | Round 5 | Round 6 |
| 月　　日 | 月　　日 | 月　　日 | 月　　日 | 月　　日 | 月　　日 |

　能は日本に現存する最古のプロの演劇です。14世紀に始まった、雅やかな音楽つきの舞踊劇です。能の舞台はおごそかな儀式のように見えます。奥深く深淵な仏教的な人生観を表現しています。演者は神の世界と人間の世界の<u>橋渡しをする者</u>です。したがって能の演目のテーマは現世の生ではありません。役者の動きはゆったりとしていて、高度に様式化されています。俳優はすべて男性で、通常は面をつけます。面は代々流派に伝えられます。俳優の演技には、謡や鼓や笛の演奏がともないます。現在のプログラムは、2つか3つの<u>能の演目</u>の間に半時間の狂言をはさんだものが普通です。

　室町時代に能を大成させた世阿弥が著した『風姿花伝』は、能の芸能論にとどまらない深さがあります。『風姿花伝』のなかの「秘すれば花なり」という言葉は、日本人ならだれでも知っているフレーズです。

　狂言は能の演目の間に演じられるコメディのようなものです。狂言は、あらゆる点で荘重な能とは対照的です。扱う素材は現実の世の中です。登場人物には駄目なところも人情もユーモアもあります。そのため、能より一般受けします。

31 文楽・盆栽 [bunraku / bonsai]
Bunraku & Bonsai

Bunraku is traditional puppet theater from the 17th century. It combines chanting of dramatic ballads (*joruri*), a three-stringed lute (*shamisen*) accompaniment and the manipulation of puppets. The plots are similar to kabuki. The puppets are from one to one and a half meters tall. They are not operated like marionettes. The principal puppeteer holds and manipulates the puppet's head and right arm. He is usually seen full face by the audience. Two hooded assistants operate the other arm and legs.

The best known bunraku play is *Kanadehon Chushingura* ("Chushingura" means The Treasury of Loyal Retainers). The story is based on a famous vendetta. The play is also performed in kabuki.

・・・・・

Bonsai, miniature potted plants and trees, are admired around the world. These small "gardens in a pot" usually have a tree, especially a pine tree, as the main item. In addition, there may be another small tree, a flower, or moss to cover the surface of the soil.

Pruning the plants and trees and shaping them with wire takes years. Exceptional bonsai may be cared for by several generations of people. Bonsai in Japan is usually a hobby for the elderly, but young people now come to Japan from overseas to learn this aesthetic art.

(206words)

Round 1	Round 2	Round 3	Round 4	Round 5	Round 6
月　日	月　日	月　日	月　日	月　日	月　日

　文楽は 17 世紀に生まれた、伝統の**人形劇**です。浄瑠璃（**物語詩**に節をつけた語り）、三味線の伴奏、人形の操作が組み合わさっています。ドラマの**筋**は歌舞伎に似ています。人形の背丈は 1 メートルから 1 メートル半です。**操り人形**のように糸で操作するのではありません。主遣いが人形を支え、頭と右手をあやつります。観客に顔がそのまま見えるのがふつうです。もう一方の手と足を 2 人の顔を隠した助手があやつります。

　文楽の演目でもっとも有名なのは、仮名手本忠臣蔵です（忠臣蔵というのは、「忠実な家臣の宝庫」という意味です）。この物語は有名な**復讐劇**がもとになっています。この演目は歌舞伎でも演じられます。

・・・・・

　盆栽はミニチュアの**鉢植え**ですが、世界中で愛好されています。この小さな「鉢の中の庭」には、中心要素として 1 本の樹木、特に松の木のあるのがふつうです。それに加えて、もう 1 本小さな木か、花か、土をおおう**苔**があしらわれることもあります。

　草や木をきちんと剪定し、針金を使って成形するには何年もかかります。親から子へと何代にもわたって世話されてきた、希少な盆栽もあります。日本の盆栽はふつうは年齢層の高い人々の趣味です。しかし、現在では、海外の若者たちが、この**美的芸術**の技を学びに日本に来ます。

32 幽霊・鬼・妖怪 [yurei / oni / yokai]
Ghosts, Demons & Goblins

Yurei, ghost, is the word for the spirit or soul of a dead person. It appears as a shadowy likeness of the deceased person. These ghosts have two characteristics. First, they have a specific reason for returning to the world of the living. Second, they can only be seen by certain people. *Yurei* are usually pictured in human form with messy hair, long dangling arms and no legs.

Bakemono are monsters, goblins and supernatural beings. All together they are called *yokai*. They appear in various nonhuman forms, usually at dusk in a specific place. Of the hundreds of types, common ones are *kappa*, *tengu* and *yamamba*. The *tengu* has a long nose, wings, a red face and a feather fan. It lives in deep mountains and has powers of illusion and possession.

Oni are ferocious horned demons. They are associated with the torturers of the Buddhist hells. However, they have another, more benevolent side which sweeps away evil influences.

Mononoke are primarily associated with the Heian period. These were "wandering spirits" of the living or dead. They were thought to possess a person and cause illness or death.

(188words)

| Round 1 | Round 2 | Round 3 | Round 4 | Round 5 | Round 6 |
| 月　　日 | 月　　日 | 月　　日 | 月　　日 | 月　　日 | 月　　日 |

「幽霊」は死んだ人の霊、もしくは魂を意味する言葉です。亡くなった人の生前の姿形で出てきますが、影のようなはかない姿です。幽霊には２つの特徴があります。１つは、生きている者たちの世界に帰ってくるための、何か特別の理由があるということです。もう１つは、その幽霊が見える人と見えない人がいるということです。幽霊はふつう、ばさばさの髪、だらりと垂らした手をしていて、足はありません。

「化け物」とは怪物、天狗などこの世ならざる生き物のことです。全部ひっくるめて「妖怪」といいます。様々な人間ならざる姿で、たそがれ時に、特定の決まった場所に現れるのがふつうです。何百種類もありますが、河童、天狗、山姥などがおなじみのものです。天狗は長い鼻と羽根があり、顔は赤く、羽うちわを持っています。山の奥に住んでいて、幻を見せたり、人をたぶらかす神通力をもっています。

「鬼」は気性のあらい、角のある魔物です。鬼というと、仏教でいう地獄で人をこらしめる者という連想が働きます。その一方で、厄払いしてくれるという親切な面をも持っています。

「もののけ」は主として平安時代と結びついています。すなわち死霊と生霊［生きている人、死んだ人の「さまよえる魂」］のことです。人に取り憑いて、病気にさせたり死なせたりするものと考えられていました。

33 浮世絵 [ukiyo-e]
Ukiyo-e

Woodblock prints (*hanga*) were an early method of making multiple copies of a story or a picture. The artist carved a wooden block leaving a design or text on the surface. Ink was spread on that surface and then a sheet of paper was laid on it. The resulting print created a reverse image of what was left uncarved on the block.

In the mid-17th century, the entertainment districts of Kyoto, Osaka and Edo developed rapidly. The word *ukiyo*, "floating world," was originally used in the sense of "this world." But in this period, it came to refer to a carefree life people enjoyed in those districts. Artists began portraying the residents and visitors in these districts in woodblock prints called *ukiyo-e*, "woodblock prints of the demimonde." Many of the early prints showed high-ranking courtesans (*tayu*). Prints of popular sumo wrestlers and kabuki actors were added later on. Around 1745, artists began using multiple woodblocks, each with a different color ink to make one picture. These *nishiki-e*, "brocade pictures," became the mainstream technique.

In the late 18th century, Utamaro and Sharaku began creating sensual prints of beautiful women. Hokusai and Hiroshige in the early 19th century produced superb landscapes, views of Edo, the Tokaido Road and Mt. Fuji. Ukiyo-e art had a major influence on Van Gogh and the Impressionists in Europe.

(222words)

Round 1	Round 2	Round 3	Round 4	Round 5	Round 6
月　　日	月　　日	月　　日	月　　日	月　　日	月　　日

　<u>版面</u>は１つの物語や絵について、多数の部数を作るために昔用いられた技法でした。製作者は木製の版木を彫り、表面に模様や文章を刻みつけます。その上にインクを塗り、１枚の紙をのせます。そうしてできる版画には、版木の彫られていなかった部分の<u>反転像</u>が写りました。

　17世紀の中頃、京都、大阪、江戸で遊里が急速に発達しました。「浮世」(「浮かんでいる世界」)はもともと「この世」という意味で用いられましたが、この時代に、遊里での気楽な人生を意味するようになりました。そこに住んでいる者や訪れる客たちのことを、画家が木版画に描くようになりました。それが浮世絵(「遊女の版画」)です。最初の頃の浮世絵には、太夫（高級娼婦）が描かれていましたが、後にこれに加えて、人気の<u>力士</u>や歌舞伎役者の浮世絵も作られるようになりました。1745年ごろ、１枚の絵をつくるためにそれぞれ異なった色を施す、複数の版木が用いられるようになり、この錦絵(「金襴の絵」)の手法が主流になりました。

　18世紀の末に、歌麿と写楽があだっぽい美人を描いた浮世絵を制作しはじめました。19世紀になると、北斎と広重が江戸や東海道や富士山を描いたみごとな風景画を生み出しました。浮世絵の作風はヴァン・ゴッホをはじめヨーロッパの<u>印象派の芸術家</u>に大きな影響をあたえました。

34 日本刀（刀） [nihonto (katana)]
Japanese Swords

The Japanese sword (*nihonto* or *katana*) first appeared in the 8th century. The Japanese quickly mastered steelmaking and used it to develop swords with graceful shapes, textures and color variations. The Japanese sword had a spiritual significance for over 12 centuries. It is even one of the three Imperial Regalia, together with the jewels and the mirror.

The blade is slightly curved, and has harder and softer sections. The blade is cross-welded and densely forged. As a result, it is made up of many layers of steel, making it extremely strong. The edge is incredibly sharp due to a complex series of polishings.

The highest quality swords were made in the Kamakura period. Most of the blades which are considered national treasures come from this period. During the Muromachi period, there was almost constant fighting, and sword-making flourished. A new practice of using long and short swords, *katana* and *wakizashi*, for combat came into fashion. In the Edo period (1603-1867), these swords became symbols of samurai status. Swordsmiths created beautiful tempering patterns on the blade and artistic sword guards (*tsuba*).

Today Japanese swords are found in museums as examples of superb Japanese craftsmanship and artistry. All privately owned swords must be registered with the police.

(205words)

| Round 1 | Round 2 | Round 3 | Round 4 | Round 5 | Round 6 |
| 月　日 | 月　日 | 月　日 | 月　日 | 月　日 | 月　日 |

　日本刀は 8 世紀に誕生しました。日本は**製鋼技術**をすばやく習得し、それによって、優美な形、肌理、色合いをそなえた刀を作り上げました。日本刀は以後 1200 年にわたって、精神的な意味合いを持ち続けました。勾玉、鏡と並んで**天皇家の三種の神器**にすらなっています。

　わずかに反っている刃の硬さは、部分によって様々です。刃は鋼を何度も折り返しながら、密に鍛えられます。その結果として多重の鋼の層ができ、きわめて強靭な鋼となります。刃は一連の複雑なプロセスによって磨かれるので、信じられないほど鋭くとがっています。

　最高の品質の刀は鎌倉時代に作られました。国宝級の刀はほとんどがこの時期のものです。室町時代は戦乱が絶えなかったので、刀作りが繁盛しました。戦いの際に刀と脇差の長短 2 本の刀を持つという、新たな風習が**流行し始めました**。江戸時代（1603 〜 1867）には、こうした刀は侍という身分のシンボルとなりました。焼戻しによる刃の美しい模様、芸術的な鍔が、**刀鍛冶**によって創り出されました。

　今日では、日本刀は、日本の卓越した**職人技**と芸術性を示すものとして博物館に所蔵されています。個人所有の刀は、すべて警察に登録しなければなりません。

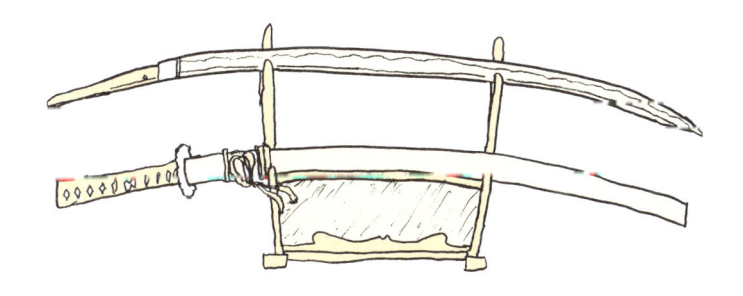

このページに、使ってみたい英語表現や、覚えておきたい英単語などを書き込んでおきましょう

Chapter 4
日本の文化

35 侍 [*samurai*]
Samurai

Samurai, or *bushi*, were the warrior elite of Japan between the 12th and the mid-19th centuries. The word "samurai" literally means "one who serves." In the beginning, they were low-ranking officials administering the provinces. In the 12th century, the first warrior government in Japan was established in Kamakura. The head of this government was given the title of generalissimo (*shogun*), by the imperial court. Basically from that time on, the samurai administered the country. Within the samurai class, each warrior had a place in a lord-vassal hierarchy.

Samurai led the fighting that lasted from 1467 until the Tokugawa shogunate brought peace in 1603. With peace, the samurai had to switch from fighting to administering. They became the ruling class and their fighting skills became less important. As a samurai was in the service of a lord (*daimyo*), the lord provided him with work and an income, and the samurai was fiercely loyal to his lord. A samurai could be dismissed from service or his lord could lose his domain. If this happened, he became a *ronin*, masterless samurai, who had no source of income.

Samurai were the only class allowed to carry two swords and wear a topknot hairstyle (*chonmage*). These two symbols of their status were both discontinued in the Meiji era.

(216words)

侍、もしくは武士は、12世紀から19世紀半ばまで日本の軍事的エリート集団でした。「侍」という語は、文字通りには「仕える者」という意味です。もともと侍というのは、地方を治めている身分の低い役人でした。12世紀に日本で初の武家の政権が鎌倉に確立されました。この政権の頂点に立つ者が、朝廷によって将軍（すなわち「最高司令官」）に任命されました。この時以降、基本的には侍が日本を統治しました。侍の身分の中で、それぞれの侍が**主従の序列**のどこかに属していました。

　1467年以降、侍が中心の戦乱の世が続きましたが、1603年、**徳川幕府**によって天下統一がなされました。平和の訪れとともに侍は戦(いくさ)から**政（まつりごと）**へと転換しなければなりませんでした。彼らは**支配階級**となり、戦いの技術はさほど重要でなくなりました。侍は大名（殿様）に仕えているので、殿様は彼らに役と禄を与え、侍は殿様に対して苛烈なまでの**忠誠心**をささげました。侍は禄を失うことがありましたし、殿様だって国を失うことがありました。もしそんなことにでもなれば、侍は浪人、すなわち「主人のいない侍」となり、収入の道が閉ざされました。

　侍は2本の刀を帯びて、ちょんまげを結うことが許された唯一の階級でした。この2つは侍の身分を示すシンボルでしたが、どちらも明治の時代になると廃止されました。

36 忍者 [ninja]
Ninja

Ninjutsu, also called *shinobi*, is a combination of spying, deception and commando skills. During the Medieval period and the Period of Warring States (1467-1590), *ninjutsu* became an important part of Japanese martial arts. During the Edo period, the Tokugawa shoguns used *ninjutsu* techniques to keep an eye on both enemies and retainers.

Ninjutsu techniques include how to secretly enter an enemy castle, carry out assassinations, make commando raids, and gather strategic information. The masters of these techniques were known as *ninja*. They developed special tools and weapons to carry out special missions in enemy territory. Their skills were a highly valued part of military operations. Famous bands of *ninja* came from rural areas of Iga (now in Mie Prefecture) and Koga (now in Shiga Prefecture).

The *ninja* were skilled in operating invisibly. Those who were not highly skilled were captured and killed, so only the skilled survived. Nowadays, the *ninja* are romantically portrayed as superheroes.

A serious practitioner of martial arts or special operations can study *ninjutsu* or *ninpo* at the Bujinkan in Noda City, Chiba Prefecture. Practitioners from abroad are even more enthusiastic about learning *ninjutsu* than those from Japan.

(191words)

Round 1	Round 2	Round 3	Round 4	Round 5	Round 6
月　　日	月　　日	月　　日	月　　日	月　　日	月　　日

　忍術（忍びとも言います）はスパイ、**謀略**、野戦術を組み合わせたものです。中世から戦国時代（1467 ～ 1590）にかけて、忍術は日本の**武術**の中で重要な一角を占めるようになりました。江戸時代には徳川家の将軍たちが忍術の技を用いて、敵と家臣の両方を監視しました。

　忍術の技の代表的なものは、いかに知られないで敵の城に忍び込むか、**刺客の仕事**をするか、ゲリラ的な襲撃をかけるか、**計略のための情報**を収集するかなどです。こうした術を習得した者が忍者です。敵地で特殊な任務を遂行するために、特殊な道具や武器が編み出されました。忍者の技能は、軍事作戦の中でも高く評価される部分です。忍者の有名な流派が、伊賀（現在の三重県）と甲賀（現在の滋賀県）の**鄙**から出ています。

　忍者は隠密のうちに行動する技にたけていました。技の未熟な者は捕らえられ殺されたので、技の優れた者のみが生き残りました。今日では、忍者はスーパーヒーローとしてロマンチックに描かれます。

　武術、あるいは**特殊作戦**を実践する人は、忍術（忍法）を千葉県野田市の武神館で学ぶことができます。日本人よりも、海外からの参加者で熱気にあふれています。

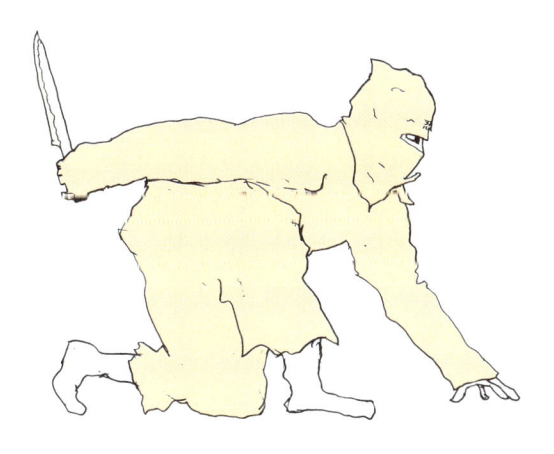

37 芸者 [geisha]
Geisha

The word geisha literally means "artist." This is an appropriate translation. Geisha are professional entertainers who have mastered many traditional Japanese arts, including dancing and playing musical instruments.

Young women begin as apprentices, called *maiko* in Kyoto and *hangyoku* in Tokyo. They live in a lodging house (*okiya*) during their training. During the day, they take lessons in Japanese dance, tea ceremony, hand drum (*tsuzumi*), a three-stringed *shamisen* and perhaps the thirteen-stringed zither (*koto*). After years of training, if they reach a certain standard in these entertainment arts, they become *geisha*.

Geisha dress in elegant kimono with an elegant wig, carefully chosen to match the occasion and the season. As a result of their long training, their every movement and their way of speaking make them consummate artists.

They are called to perform in exclusive banquet facilities (*chaya*) and Japanese-style restaurants called *ryotei*. Being entertained by a real geisha is a unique experience and not possible for most people. First of all, being entertained by a geisha is extremely expensive. Second, it is impossible to enter most of the places where they perform without a personal recommendation by a regular patron. If you want to see a geisha, you will have to try to catch one leaving a *chaya* on her way home.

(214words)

| Round 1 | Round 2 | Round 3 | Round 4 | Round 5 | Round 6 |
| 月　　日 | 月　　日 | 月　　日 | 月　　日 | 月　　日 | 月　　日 |

「芸者」という語は文字通りには「アーチスト」を意味します。この翻訳はまさにぴったりです。芸者というのは、踊りや楽器の演奏を含めた日本の伝統芸能の多くを身につけたプロの芸人だからです。

　若い女性はまず見習いとなります。京都では舞妓、東京では半玉と呼ばれます。見習い期間中は置屋に住み込みます。日中は、日本舞踊、茶の湯、鼓、3本の弦の三味線、それにあるいは琴（弦が13本のツィター）のお稽古に行きます。数年の修行の後、こうした座敷芸が一定のレベルに達すれば、芸者となります。

　芸者は、シックな着物を着て、シックな鬘(かつら)を被ります。これらは宴席と季節に合うよう念入りに選ばれています。長い修行を積んでいるので、芸者の身のこなしの1つ1つ、言葉の端々が、まさに最高のアーチストそのものです。

　芸者は茶屋（高級な宴会場）や料亭（日本式レストラン）に呼ばれていって芸を披露します。本物の芸者にもてなされることは特殊な経験であり、ほとんどの人にはできないことです。まず第一に、芸者さんに接待してもらうと、たいへんな高額になります。第二に、彼女たちが演じるほとんどの場所には、常連のひいき客による個人的な推薦がなければ入ることができません。もし、芸者が見たいなら、お茶屋から家路につくところをつかまえるしかありません。

38 日本語 [nihongo]
Japanese Language

The Japanese and Chinese languages are not directly related, but the Japanese writing system uses Chinese characters (*kanji*). *Kanji* came to Japan in about the 6th century. From that period on, a complex writing system developed.

First, the Chinese characters were read by their Chinese-derived pronunciation (*onyomi*). Then, the characters were used to represent the Japanese equivalent. This gave a second reading called *kunyomi*. There may be multiple *onyomi* and *kunyomi* for each character.

In addition, simplified forms of the characters were used to represent the sounds of Japanese words. Two syllabaries (*kana*) were created to be used phonetically. The cursive script is called *hiragana* and the angular script is called *katakana*.

In modern Japanese, the *hiragana* script is used together with *kanji* for writing Japanese. *Katakana* is used to write loanwords from Western languages, onomatopoeic words, and words that are emphasized.

Japanese can be written vertically from top to bottom or horizontally from left to right. Horizontally written books such as those on scientific matters open in the Western manner from right to left. Newspapers and other books open from left to right.

(184words)

Round 1	Round 2	Round 3	Round 4	Round 5	Round 6
月　　日	月　　日	月　　日	月　　日	月　　日	月　　日

　日本語と中国語に直接の関係はありませんが、日本語の文字は中国語に由来します。6世紀ごろ、**中国語の文字**（漢字）が日本にもたらされました。その時以来、**複雑な文字体系**が発達してきました。

　まず、漢字が中国語に由来する音（音読み）で読まれました。次いで、漢字は、その漢字の意味と同義の日本語を表すのに用いられました。これによって訓読みという、2つ目の読み方が誕生しました。それぞれの漢字に対して、複数の音読みと訓読みが存在するものもあります。

　これに加えて、日本語の音を表すために、漢字を単純化したものが用いられました。音を表すのに、2種類のカナ（音節文字体系）が創り出されました。このうち**丸みのある文字**はヒラガナと呼ばれ、**角ばった文字**はカタカナと呼ばれます。

　現代の日本語では、文字で表すときには、ヒラガナと漢字が組み合わせて用いられます。カタカナは外来語（西洋語からの借用語）や**擬声語・擬音語**、強調したい語を記すときに使われます。

　日本語は上から下へ縦書き、あるいは左から右へ横書きすることができます。科学の本のように横書きで書かれている本は、西洋式に右から左へと開きます。新聞やその他の本は、左から右へと開きます。

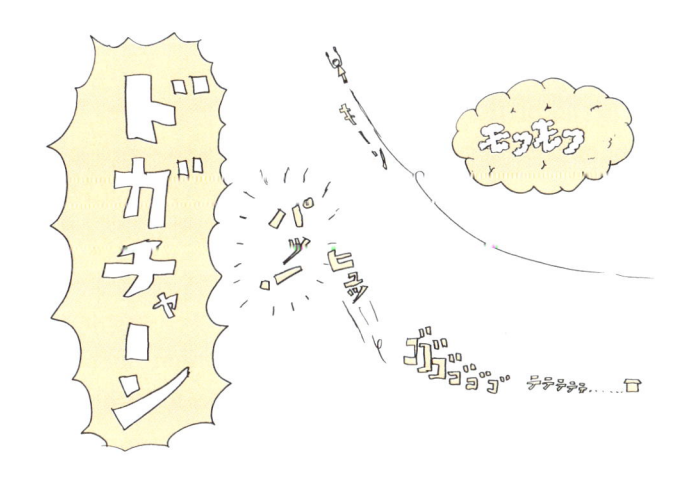

39 日本庭園 [nihon teien]
Japanese Gardens

Japanese gardens (*nihon teien*) combine and synthesize a variety of elements. They have been created since the Heian period. They incorporate natural trees, plants, flowers, water, rocks and sand to create a landscape and show seasonal changes. Japanese gardens contrast with Western gardens in not aiming for symmetry. To the contrary, Japanese gardens try to mimic natural landscapes within a small space.

Some gardens feature groups of rocks and raked gravel or sand. Rock and sand gardens created to look like landscapes with water are called *karesansui* gardens. Other gardens focus on flowing water or a pond with carp leisurely swimming in it.

Sometimes there is a teahouse in the garden. Stone lanterns may line the stepping-stones that lead to the teahouse.

In addition, *Jodoshiki teien*, under the influence of the idea of the Buddhist paradise, represent the Pure Land of Amida Buddha. Famous examples are the garden at Motsuji temple in Hiraizumi, Iwate Prefecture, a World Heritage Site, and the garden at Byodoin temple at Uji, Kyoto Prefecture, which is depicted on the 10-yen coin.

The three most famous large landscape gardens are Korakuen (Okayama Prefecture), Kairakuen (Ibaraki Prefecture) and Kenrokuen (Ishikawa Prefecture). Major temples in Kyoto and elsewhere often have beautiful gardens as well.

(206words)

Round 1	Round 2	Round 3	Round 4	Round 5	Round 6
月　　日	月　　日	月　　日	月　　日	月　　日	月　　日

　日本庭園には様々な要素が組み合わされ、統合されています。日本庭園が造られるようになったのは平安時代からです。自然の樹木、草、花、水、岩、砂を集めて風景が作られ、**四季折々の変化**が表わされます。日本庭園は**対称形**をねらわないという点で、西洋式の庭園とは対照的です。逆に、日本庭園は小さな空間の中に自然の景観を**まねよう**とします。

　岩を配し、熊手の跡をつけた砂利や砂でできている庭園があります。岩と砂で水のある風景をイメージした庭園を「枯山水」といいます。これに対して、水を流したり、池があり**鯉**が悠然と泳いでいる庭園もあります。

　庭園の中に**茶室**があるものもあります。**石灯籠**が茶室へ向かう飛び石にならんで配されていたりします。

　他には、仏教の浄土思想の影響を受け、極楽浄土を再現しようとした浄土式庭園があります。世界遺産にもなっている岩手県平泉の毛越寺、10円硬貨に描かれている京都府宇治の平等院などが有名です。

　風景式の3大庭園は後楽園（岡山県）、偕楽園（茨城県）、兼六園（石川県）です。京都などの有名寺院には美しい庭園のある場合が多いです。

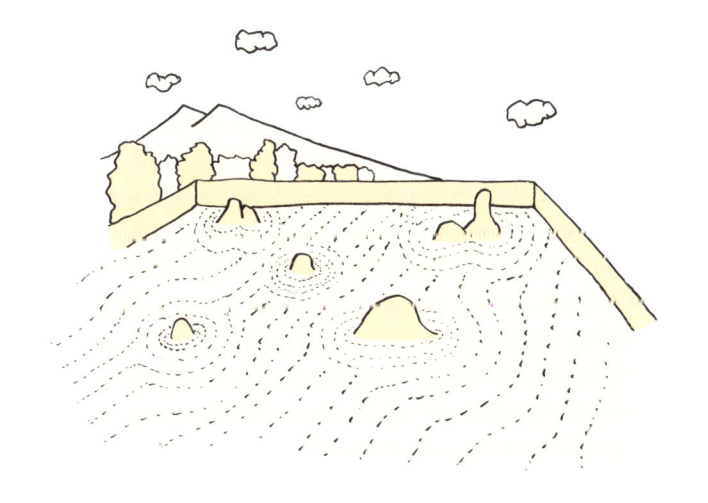

40 国歌・国花・国鳥・国旗
[*kokka / kokka / kokucho / kokki*]
National Anthem, Flower, Bird, and Flag

"*Kimi-ga-yo*" is Japan's national anthem (*kokka*). It has no official English title, but it is usually translated as "His Majesty's Reign." The lyrics are taken from "Collection from Ancient and Modern Times" (*Kokinwakashu*), a 10th-century collection of Japanese poems. The music was composed in 1880, and it became the official national anthem in 1999.

Japan does not have an official national flower. However, the flower that symbolizes Japan is the cherry blossom (*sakura*). The chrysanthemum (*kiku*) is the symbol of the Imperial Household. The imperial crest is a chrysanthemum with 16 petals. The green pheasant or Japanese pheasant (*kiji*) is the national bird.

The national flag is called the *Hinomaru*, which means "circle of the sun." It is a red circle on a white background. *Nihon* (Japan) basically means the land of the rising sun, so the red circle is symbolic of the sun. Incidentally, the same design is used on the national flag of Bangladesh, a red circle on a green background, and on that of Palau, a yellow circle on a bright blue background.

(173words)

Round 1	Round 2	Round 3	Round 4	Round 5	Round 6
月　日	月　日	月　日	月　日	月　日	月　日

　日本の国歌は「君が代」です。正式な英語名はありませんが、"His Majesty's Reign"（陛下の御代）と訳されるのがふつうです。詞は10世紀の日本の歌集『古今和歌集』からのものです。1880年に曲がつけられ、1999年に正式に国歌となりました。

　日本には公式には国花はありません。しかし日本を象徴する花は桜です。菊は天皇家のシンボルです。天皇家の紋章は16八重表菊（16の花弁のある菊）です。緑の雉（日本雉）が国鳥です。

　国旗は日の丸と呼ばれます。「太陽の丸」という意味です。白の背景に赤い丸です。「日本」は「昇る日の国」という意味なので、赤い丸は太陽を象徴しています。ちなみに、同じデザインで、緑に赤丸だとバングラデシュ、明るい青に黄丸だとパラオの国旗になります。

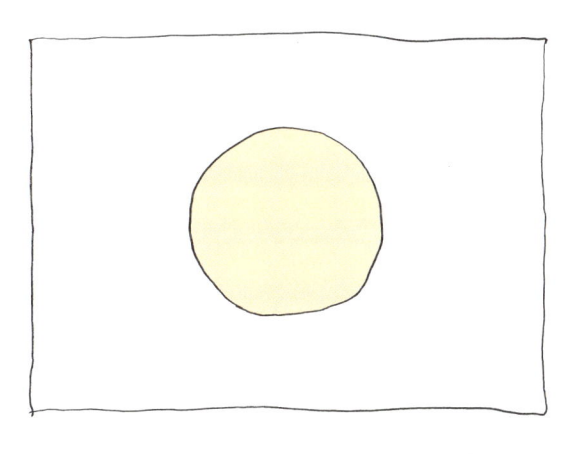

君が代は
千代に八千代に
さざれ石の
いわおとなりて
こけのむすまで

41 旧暦 [kyuureki]
The Old Japanese Calendar

Until 1872, Japan used an ancient calendar for the months. For example *risshun* (the beginning of spring) in the 2015 calendar was February 4. The names of special days in the old calendar are still important in traditional poetry. They are called *nijuyon sekki*. Even today, people are still aware of them and weather forecasts sometimes mention these names.

(68words)

The Twenty-four Points (Sekki) of the Old Solar Calendar (dates are for 2015)

Old Solar Calendar	Contemporary Calendar	Name of Sekki	Basic Meaning
January	4 February	Risshun	Beginning of spring
	19 February	Usui	Rainwater
February	6 March	Keichitsu	Insects emerge
	21 March	Shumbun	Vernal equinox
March	5 April	Seimei	Pure and clear
	20 April	Kokuu	Grain rains
April	6 May	Rikka	Beginning of summer
	21 May	Shoman	Growth of living things
May	6 June	Boshu	Grain seeds
	22 June	Geshi	Summer solstice
June	7 July	Shosho	Lesser heat
	23 July	Taisho	Greater heat
July	8 August	Risshu	Beginning of autumn
	23 August	Shosho	Lessening of heat
August	8 September	Hakuro	White dew
	23 September	Shubun	Autumnal equinox
September	8 October	Kanro	Cold dew
	24 October	Soko	Frost falls
Octorbber	8 November	Ritto	Beginning of winter
	23 November	Shosetsu	Light snow
November	7 December	Taisetsu	Great snow
	22 December	Toji	Winter solstice
December	6 January	Shokan	Lesser cold
	20 January	Daikan	Greater cold

Round 1	Round 2	Round 3	Round 4	Round 5	Round 6
月　日	月　日	月　日	月　日	月　日	月　日

1872年まで、日本では旧暦によって1年の月を表していました。例えば、立春（春の始まり）は、2015年のカレンダーでは2月4日です。旧暦の中の特別な日の名前は、今でも詩歌において重要です。二十四節気といいます。今日でさえ旧暦は人々に意識されており、天気予報の際に、旧暦の日の名前に触れることがあります。

二十四節気（日付は2015年のもの）

旧暦一月	立春（2月4日）	雨水（2月19日）
旧暦二月	啓蟄（3月6日）	春分（3月21日）
旧暦三月	清明（4月5日）	穀雨（4月20日）
旧暦四月	立夏（5月6日）	小満（5月21日）
旧暦五月	芒種（6月6日）	夏至（6月22日）
旧暦六月	小暑（7月7日）	大暑（7月23日）
旧暦七月	立秋（8月8日）	処暑（8月23日）
旧暦八月	白露（9月8日）	秋分（9月23日）
旧暦九月	寒露（10月8日）	霜降（10月24日）
旧暦十月	立冬（11月8日）	小雪（11月23日）
旧暦十一月	大雪（12月7日）	冬至（12月22日）
旧暦十二月	小寒（1月6日）	大寒（1月20日）

42 六曜・十二支(干支) [rokuyo / junishi (eto)]
Rokuyo & The Twelve Animals of the Zodiac

In the old Japanese calendar, six designations of fortune were added to the days. This was a guide to days that were auspicious and inauspicious. Even now, people often avoid holding a wedding on *butsumetsu*, because that day is considered inauspicious. Instead, people prefer *taian*, because that day is the most auspicious of the cycle.

The six-day cycle consists of *sensho* (morning is lucky), *tomobiki* (an unfortunate day for a funeral), *sembu* (afternoon is lucky), *butsumetsu* (all day is unlucky), *taian* (all day is lucky for celebrations), and *shakko* (unlucky in all respects).

. . . . .

Japan uses the Chinese zodiac of twelve animals. New Year greeting cards usually have that year's animal as part of the design. Most Japanese know which of these the current year is.

Japanese often comment that a person has characteristics of the animal of the year when he or she was born. People born in the year of the ox (*ushi*) [2009, 1997, 1985, 1973, 1961, 1949, 1937], for example, are supposed to be patient and enduring, and to inspire confidence in others.

(178words)

Round 1	Round 2	Round 3	Round 4	Round 5	Round 6
月　日	月　日	月　日	月　日	月　日	月　日

　日本の旧暦で、運勢を表す 6 つの表記が日付につけられるようになりました。これは縁起の善い日と悪い日を教えてくれる指針でした。現在でも、仏滅は不吉とされているので、その日の結婚式は避けられることが多いです。代わりに大安が好まれます。大安の日は六曜の中でもっとも縁起がよいからです。

　六曜とは、先勝（午前中は吉）、友引（葬式に不向き）、先負（午後は吉）、仏滅（終日凶）、大安（全日、祝い事によし）、赤口（万事に凶）です。

・・・・・

　日本は、**12 の動物からなる中国の十二支**を使います。年賀状では通常、その年の動物がデザインの一部になっています。今年の干支は何か、たいていの日本人は知っています。

　日本人はよく、人は自分の干支の動物と性質が同じだと言います。例えば、丑（牛）の年 [2009、1997、1985、1973、1961、1949、1937] に生まれた人は、気が長く、粘り強い性格で、信頼感があるとされています。

Chinese zodiac of 12 animals	**十二支**	
ne (rat, mouse)	子	鼠
ushi (ox)	丑	牛
tora (tiger)	寅	虎
u (rabbit)	卯	兎
tatsu (dragon)	辰	竜
mi (snake)	巳	蛇
uma (horse)	午	馬
hitsuji (sheep)	未	羊
saru (monkey)	申	猿
tori (rooster)	酉	鶏
inu (dog)	戌	犬
i (boar)	亥	猪

43 金魚・錦鯉・鯉のぼり
[kingyo / nishikigoi / koinobori]
Goldfish, Brocade Carp & Carp Streamers

Japanese enjoy keeping goldfish (*kingyo*) in glass bowls. *Kingyo* sellers once flourished in Tokyo. They carried buckets of these little fish suspended from a carrying pole over their shoulder. These sellers are gone, but at summer festivals, there are often street stalls for "scooping goldfish" (*kingyo sukui*). These have plastic pools filled with goldfish. The customer dips a paper-covered wire loop into the water and tries to scoop up as many goldfish as he can. Once the paper tears, the game is over. It's not as easy as it sounds. The successful customer gets to take the goldfish home. To scoop up a goldfish without the paper tearing requires considerable skill.

Nishikigoi can be described as "brocade carp" because of their fancy coloring. Some Japanese gardens (*nihon teien*) have ponds with these multi-colored carp swimming in them. Certain varieties of *nishikigoi* are extremely expensive to purchase.

Koinobori are streamers with designs of carp that are displayed during the traditional Boys' Festival in May (*Tango no sekku*). *Koi* means carp, and *nobori* means streamer or banner. This is now celebrated on May 5th as Children's Day. The day is a time to pray for the health and happiness of children.

(200words)

| Round 1 | Round 2 | Round 3 | Round 4 | Round 5 | Round 6 |
| 月　　　日 | 月　　　日 | 月　　　日 | 月　　　日 | 月　　　日 | 月　　　日 |

　日本人は金魚をガラス鉢で飼うのが好きです。東京では昔、金魚売りが繁盛しました。金魚を入れたバケツを、肩にかついだ担い棒につるして持ってきたものです。そんな金魚売りはもういなくなってしまいました。しかし夏のお祭りによく露天の店が出て、金魚すくいができます。プラスチックプールに、金魚がいっぱい入っています。お客は紙をはった輪っか（ポイ）を水につけて、金魚をできるだけ数多くすくおうとします。紙が破れてしまったら終了です。簡単そうに聞こえますが、けっこうむずかしいです。うまくすくった人は、金魚をもらって帰ります。紙が破れないように金魚をすくって水から上げるには、かなりの腕前が必要です。

　錦鯉はあでやかな色をしているので、「金襴［錦］の鯉」という言い方がぴったりかもしれません。日本の庭園では、このような色とりどりの鯉が池で泳いでいることがあります。錦鯉は種類によってはとても高価なものもあります。

「鯉のぼり」というのは、5月の端午の節句（昔の「男の子のお祭り」）の間に飾る、鯉を型どった吹き流しです。「こい」は "carp" のことで、「のぼり」は吹き流しもしくは旗のことです。今では5月5日に「こどもの日」として祝います。その日は、子どもの健康と幸せを祈る日なのです。

44 相撲 [sumo]
Sumo

Sumo is a form of Japanese wrestling that began in ancient times. Originally it was an agricultural rite. Even now, some Shinto shrines perform sumo as a ritual. It has been a professional sport since the Edo period. Today it is practiced by clubs in high schools and universities and by amateur groups. The most popular competitions are the 15-day tournaments held by the Japan Sumo Association. These tournaments begin on a Sunday in the odd-numbered months and end two Sundays later. Tokyo hosts the January, May, and September tournaments. The other tournaments are held in Osaka (March), Nagoya (July) and Fukuoka (November).

Bouts take place in the circular *dohyo*, a pounded-clay ring. Women are forbidden to enter the ring. A wrestler can win in two ways. One is to force his opponent out of the ring. The second is to cause him to touch the surface of the ring with any part of his body except the bottom of his feet. A referee and five judges decide the winner.

Each wrestler wears a belt called a *mawashi*. The competitors try to grasp this belt and lift, push, twist or pull the opponent out of the ring or to the ground.

(194words)

Round 1	Round 2	Round 3	Round 4	Round 5	Round 6
月　　　日	月　　　日	月　　　日	月　　　日	月　　　日	月　　　日

　相撲は古代に起源のある日本式のレスリングです。もともとは、農耕儀礼として行われていました。現在でも、神事として相撲を行っている神社もあります。江戸時代にプロスポーツとなり、現代では高校や大学のクラブ、そしてアマチュアのサークルでも行われています。様々な競技会がありますが、もっとも人気あるのは、日本相撲協会によって行われている15日間の興行です。奇数月の日曜日にはじまり、2週間後の日曜日に終わります。1月、5月、9月は東京で行われます。残りは大阪（3月）、名古屋（7月）、福岡（11月）です。

　勝負は円形の土俵（すなわち粘土を搗きかためたリング）の中で行われます。土俵は女人禁制です。勝ち方は2つあります。相手を土俵の外に出すのが1つです。もう1つは、足の裏以外の相手の体のいずれかの部分を土俵につけさせることです。行事と5人の審判が勝者を判定します。

　どの力士も回しと呼ばれる帯を巻いています。力士はこの回しをつかんで、相手を持ち上げたり、押したり、ひねったり、引いたりして土俵から出すか、相手に土をつけようとします。

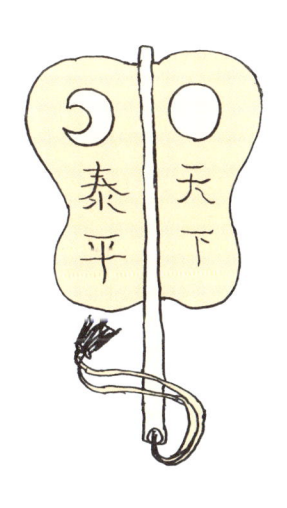

武道 [budo]
Japanese Martial Arts

Historically, the specific martial arts (*bujutsu*) practiced by the samurai included *kendo* (Japanese fencing), judo, *kyudo* (Japanese archery), *iaido* (sword drawing from a sitting position), *naginata* (halberd), and *ninjutsu* techniques.

In the Edo period (1603-1868), however, warriors had little actual fighting to do, so they practiced martial arts in ways that were not lethal. Instead of preparing for individual combat, these samurai studied strategy and learned how to administer the domains. After the Meiji Restoration (1868), the warrior class no longer needed the martial arts and other classes of people began to participate in those arts. Gradually *bujutsu* was replaced by *budo*.

Today *budo*, "the martial way," includes spiritual development as well as fighting arts. Development of physical skills provides opportunities for competition, so these arts may seem like sports. But through the traditional *budo*, a person seeks self-discipline and respect for others. The person aims for a rigorous spirit that goes beyond victory or defeat. In this sense, "the martial way" is a means of developing moral judgment and achieving self-mastery. It is a physical means toward a spiritual end.

(181words)

元来、特に侍がたしなんだ武術としては、剣道（日本流フェンシング）、柔道、弓道（日本流アーチェリー）、居合道（座った姿勢から刀を抜く）、なぎなた（鉾槍）、忍術などがありました。

　ところが江戸時代（1603〜1868）になると、侍は実際に戦う必要はほとんどありませんでした。彼らは武術を、相手が死なないような形で鍛錬しました。こうした侍たちは、個人と個人が戦うための鍛錬ではなく、兵法を学び、まつりごとを学びました。明治維新（1868）後、士族にとって武道はもはや無用の長物となり、むしろそれ以外の階級の人々がそうした技芸に手を染めるようになりました。こうして次第に武術が武道へと変わっていったのです。

　今日の「武道」、すなわち「武術の道」には、戦いの技術だけでなく、**精神修養**も含まれます。肉体の技能を磨くと、人との競い合いの場が生じてきます。したがって、こうした技芸はスポーツのように見えるかもしれません。しかし、**自己修練**と人へのうやまいを追求するのが本来の武道です。勝ち負けを超越する不動の精神を目指すのです。その意味で、武道は人としての正しい判断力を鍛える手段、自我を超越するための手段です。肉体によって、精神を高めるためのものなのです。

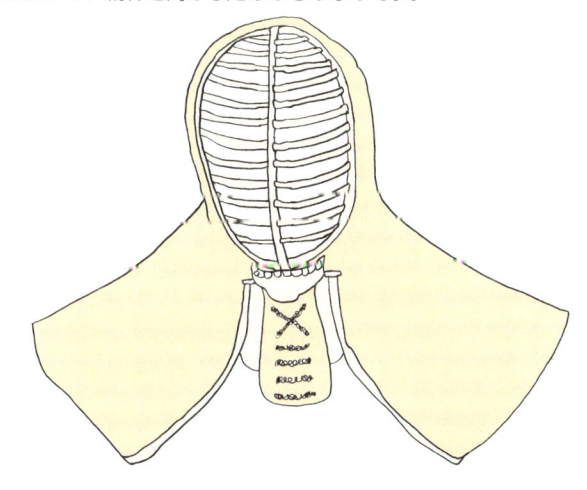

46 松竹梅／風呂敷 [*shochikubai / furoshiki*]
Pine, Bamboo and Plum / Wrapping Cloths

The names of three plants—pine, bamboo, and plum trees—make the phrase *sho-chiku-bai*. All three are able to endure harsh cold weather. The pine remains green all through the winter. The bamboo bends under heavy snows without breaking. The plum is usually the first tree to bloom as winter comes to an end. Together they are used for New Year decorations. At New Year's, bamboo and pine decorations (*kadomatsu*) are placed at entrances to houses and office buildings, and plum blossoms are used in decorations at the beginning of spring.

The phrase *shochikubai* is an expression used for other auspicious events such as weddings. Together they symbolize steadfastness, perseverance and resilience. This is just what one needs to make a marriage work.

· · · · ·

Furoshiki are square cloths of various sizes that were traditionally used to wrap and carry things. They can be made of cotton, silk or synthetic materials and are both convenient and visually attractive. They also make charming gifts because of their unique designs.

The standard wrapping technique is to put the object in the middle and tie the opposite corners together. This is convenient for keeping clothes together inside a suitcase. More advanced techniques allow one to wrap wine bottles and round objects like melons.

(211words)

Round 1	Round 2	Round 3	Round 4	Round 5	Round 6
月　　日	月　　日	月　　日	月　　日	月　　日	月　　日

　３つの植物 - **松**、**竹**、**梅** - の名で、「松竹梅」という１つの言い回しができています。どれも厳しい寒さに耐えることができる植物です。松は冬中青々としています。竹は大雪が上につもっても、しなって折れることがありません。梅は冬が終わると、ふつう真っ先に花を開く木です。新年のおめでたい飾りに、これら３つが合わさって用いられます。新年には、家々やオフィスの入り口に、竹と松をあしらった門松が置かれます。梅の花は、初春の飾りに用いられます。

　松竹梅という表現は、その他結婚式などの**めでたい場**でも用いられます。この３つ組は、堅実さ、我慢強さ、柔軟さを象徴しています。これは結婚生活をうまく続かせるのに、まさになくてはならないものでしょう。

・・・・・

「風呂敷」は様々なサイズの**四角い布**です。昔からものを包んだりもち運んだりするのに用いられてきました。コットン、シルク、合成繊維などでできていて、とても便利です。それに見た目もすてきです。珍しいデザインなので、すてきな贈り物にもなります。

　標準的な包み方としては、真ん中にものを置き、向かい合った角を結び合わせます。スーツケースの中で衣類がばらけないようにしておくのに重宝します。ワインボトルやメロンのような**丸いもの**を包む、もっと上級の技術もあります。

47 畳 [tatami]
Tatami Mats

A tatami is a mat used as flooring in traditional Japanese-style rooms. In traditional homes, almost every room had tatami flooring. Now, however, only one room might have this matting, or perhaps none at all. Each mat has a thick straw base covered with a softer woven rush. The mats within each region are a standard size, but that size differs by region.

Overall, the average size is approximately 180 cm by 90 cm. Mats are about 6 cm thick. The size of the mat is used as a unit of measure, even for rooms with no tatami. The character for *tatami* is also read *jo*. Therefore a room that has floor space for eight mats is called a *hachijo* ("eight-mat" room). An eight-mat room in Kyoto is bigger than one in Tokyo, because the mat size is larger.

In this connection, rooms in Japanese apartments and houses are also described by the letters L, D, and K with numbers. A 2LDK apartment has 2 bedrooms (2) and a combined living room (L), dining room (D) and kitchen (K).

Tokyo has the reputation of having the highest rents in the world, but actually Tokyo rents are lower than Singapore, London, New York and Hong Kong.

(205words)

Round 1	Round 2	Round 3	Round 4	Round 5	Round 6
月　　日	月　　日	月　　日	月　　日	月　　日	月　　日

　畳は和室の床に用いられるマットです。昔の家では、ほとんどの部屋も畳の床でした。しかし今では、畳を敷いているのは1部屋だけとか、まったくないこともあります。畳は1枚ごとに、分厚い藁の土台の上に、柔らかない草の織物が被せられています。地方ごとに標準サイズがあります。しかし、サイズは地方によって差があります。

　全体で見ると、平均サイズはおよそ180cm×90cmです。畳の厚みは約6cmです。畳のこのサイズは広さを述べる単位になっています。畳を敷いていない部屋にも用いられます。「畳」という漢字は、「じょう」とも読めます。したがって、畳8つの床スペースがある部屋は、「8畳」（8つの畳の部屋）と呼ばれます。京都の8畳の部屋は東京の8畳の部屋より大きいです。畳のサイズが大きいからです。

　ちなみに、日本のアパートや家屋の部屋は、L、D、Kに数字を付ける形でも表されます。「2LDKのアパート」というと、2つの寝室（2）と、リビング（L）とダイニング（D）とキッチン（K）を合わせた部屋があるということです。

　世界一高いといわれる東京の家賃ですが、シンガポール、ロンドン、ニューヨーク、香港よりは安いようです。

48 七福神 [shichifukujin]
Seven Deities of Good Fortune

The Seven Deities of Good Fortune became popular during the 15th through 17th centuries. They include Hindu, Buddhist and Taoist deities and sages from India, China and Japan. They are usually pictured riding in a treasure ship (*takarabune*).

Bishamonten (India) is the god of warriors and brings wealth and fortune. Daikokuten (India) protects crops and the kitchen. This deity is often shown with a magic mallet and mice, which increase in number during a good harvest. Benzaiten (India), the only female deity, is the patron of music, eloquence and the arts.

Fukurokuju (China) is the deity of long life and happiness. He carries a long staff and a scroll which is the symbol of wisdom. Hotei (China) is the deity of happiness and fortune. He is also called the Laughing Buddha in Chinese, and rubbing his big stomach is said to bring good luck. Jurojin (China) brings long life and good fortune. He has a long staff and fan and is followed by a deer, which is the symbol of longevity.

Ebisu (Japan) protects fishermen but is also believed to protect business and wealth. He is often shown with a sea bream (*tai*) which symbolizes celebration.

There is a popular walking course in the Nihonbashi area of Tokyo devoted to these seven deities, *Shichifukujin meguri*.

(212words)

Round 1	Round 2	Round 3	Round 4	Round 5	Round 6
月　　日	月　　日	月　　日	月　　日	月　　日	月　　日

　七福神は 15 世紀から 17 世紀にかけて人気が出てきました。インド、中国、日本が起源の、ヒンズー教、仏教、道教の神や賢者が含まれています。七福神は、たいてい、宝船に乗っている姿で描かれます。

　毘沙門天（インド）は戦いの神で、財福富貴を持ってきてくれます。大黒天（インド）は作物と台所の守り神です。打出の小槌と鼠がよくいっしょに描かれます。鼠は豊作の時に増えるからです。弁財天（インド）は紅一点で、音楽、弁才、技芸の神です。

　福禄寿（中国）は長寿招福の神です。長い杖と、知恵の象徴である巻物を持っています。布袋（中国）は招運来福の神です。中国語では「笑仏」と呼ばれており、布袋の大きなお腹を撫でるとご利益があると言われています。寿老人（中国）は、長寿と招運の神です。長い杖と扇を持っており、鹿を従えています。この鹿は長寿のシンボルです。

　恵比寿（日本）は漁業の神ですが、商売と財産を守るとも言われています。祝い事の象徴である、鯛を持った姿で描かれることが多いです。

　東京の日本橋界隈には、七福神にちなんで作られた散歩コース（七福神めぐり）があり、人気です。

49 温泉／招き猫 [onsen / manekineko]
Hot Springs / Welcoming Cat

Onsen, hot springs, were traditionally places for public bathing. They gradually developed into destinations for tourism. Today hot springs may be privately owned or run by towns, traditional inns, or hotels. They attract couples, families, and coworkers looking for a way to relax. Baths can be found both indoors as well as outdoors (*rotenburo*).

To be considered an *onsen*, a water source must be at least 25℃, but if too cool, the water is heated up to bath temperature. It also must have at least one of 19 specific mineral elements. Hot springs are believed to provide relief for various physical conditions. They are utilized in treating, for example, rheumatism, hypertension, nerve pain and chronic diseases of the digestive tract.

Onsen can be found throughout Japan. In fact, in 2014, a hot spring was tapped in Otemachi, the heart of Tokyo's business district. Well-known hot spring resorts include Beppu (Oita Prefecture), Atami (Shizuoka Prefecture), Kusatsu (Gunma Prefecture) and Sukayu (Aomori Prefecture).

・・・・・

A *maneki-neko* is a common figure of a cat with one paw raised. The paw is making a common Japanese beckoning gesture. It beckons customers to drinking and eating places. The name is literally "beckoning cat" but "welcoming cat" is easier to understand. A cute *maneki-neko* makes a unique souvenir.

(213words)

昔の温泉は公衆浴場でした。それが次第に**観光旅行**の行き先となってきました。今日では、温泉は個人が所有することも、町や旅館やホテルが経営していることもあります。カップル、家族の集まり、職場の同僚などでゆっくりすごすために温泉に行きます。屋内の風呂も露天風呂もあります。

　正式に温泉と呼ばれるためには、源泉が摂氏 25 度以上でなければなりません。入浴に冷たすぎる場合は、適温まで温められます。また、指定された 19 種類のミネラルのうち、少なくとも 1 種類は含まれていなければなりません。温泉は、様々な体の症状に効くと考えられています。例えばリューマチ、高血圧、神経痛、腸の慢性病などの治療に利用されています。

　温泉は日本中のほとんどどこにでもあります。2014 年には、東京のビジネス街の中心である大手町で温泉が出たほどです。有名な温泉の保養地としては別府（大分県）、熱海（静岡県）、草津（群馬県）、酸ヶ湯（青森県）などがあります。

・・・・・

　招き猫はどちらかの手を持ちあげた、おなじみの姿の猫です。この手は日本ではごくふつうの、人を手招きするときの格好です。飲み屋や食堂に入るよう、お客においでおいでしているのです。招き猫という名は文字通りには「**手招きする猫**」という意味ですが、「**歓迎する猫**」と言ったほうが分かりやすいでしょう。かわいい招き猫は、珍しいおみやげになるでしょう。

50 日本の四季 [nihon no shiki]
Japan's Four Seasons

The Japanese people are generally attuned to the changing of the seasons. Some think that only Japan has four distinct seasons, which is, of course, not true. Japanese follow the seasons by making use of the flowers of the season and pay attention to fruits, vegetables and fish that are in season.

Around the beginning of April, different varieties of cherry blossoms (*sakura*), appear. In one form or another, almost everyone goes to do *hanami*, which means "looking at flowers." In this case "flower" (*hana*) always means cherry blossoms. *Hanami* can refer to strolling under the cherry trees on a walk. It can refer to taking an excursion into a part of the country that is famous for cherry trees. Often it refers to gathering in parks like Ueno or Yoyogi with thousands of other people. They sit on plastic sheets, have drinks and snacks and enjoy themselves under the flowering trees.

In the autumn, *momiji* (autumn leaves) draw people to the mountains, parks and Japanese gardens. The word *momiji* refers to Japanese maples, but it also refers to "the changing colors of the trees" in this season.

(186words)

| Round 1 | Round 2 | Round 3 | Round 4 | Round 5 | Round 6 |
| 月　　日 | 月　　日 | 月　　日 | 月　　日 | 月　　日 | 月　　日 |

　一般に日本人は**四季折々の変化**にうまく順応しています。4つの季節がはっきりと分かれているのは日本だけだという人がいますが、言うまでもなくそれは真実ではありません。でも、日本人は季節の花をうまく用い、旬の果物、野菜、魚に心を配ります。

　4月のはじめごろ、様々な種類の**桜**が開花します。ほとんどすべての人が、何らかのかたちで花見に出かけます。この場合の「花」は常に桜を指します。花見というのは、ただ桜の下の歩道をぶらぶらすることかもしれませんが、桜の名所に出かけていくことを指すこともあります。しかし、上野公園や代々木公園の数千人の人だかりの中に出かけることを意味することが多いです。ビニールシートの上に座って、花の下でお酒を飲んだり軽食を食べたりして楽しみます。

　秋には、人々はもみじ（紅葉）を見に、山や公園や日本庭園に出かけます。「もみじ」というのは**日本の楓**のことですが、この季節に「変化する木々の色合い」を意味することもあります。

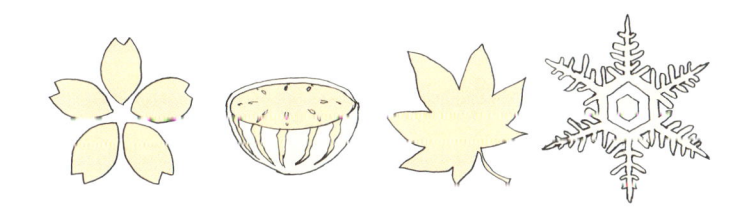

このページに、使ってみたい英語表現や、覚えておきたい英単語などを書き込んでおきましょう

Chapter 5
日本の社会

51 交通システム [kotsu shisutemu]
Transportation System

Japan's transportation system is unique in many ways. The Tokyo area has high-density transportation with 25 JR lines, 15 subway lines, 38 private railway lines, and 3 monorail lines, for a total of 81 lines. The JR lines alone carry more than 16 million passengers per day. Despite the highly complicated congested schedules, trains are amazingly punctual. Tokyo's subways, called *Metro*, are clean, smooth and highly efficient. With trains running every 3-5 minutes, you wonder why some people race to jump on even as the doors are closing. If a train is running behind schedule, even a few minutes, the conductor will make repeated apologies for the delay. The rush hour trains are packed with commuters. Many who are seated are sound asleep. Most who are standing are playing games on their mobile phones.

Japan's high-speed trains are called *Shinkansen*. In English they are sometimes called "bullet trains" because of the shape of the front of the train. The *Shinkansen* is an extremely convenient way to get from one major city to another. These trains are so punctual that they arrive and depart on the second. Over most parts of the country they run at speeds of up to 320 kilometers per hour.

(203words)

日本の交通システムは様々な点で世界に類を見ません。東京圏には、JR25路線、地下鉄15路線、私鉄38路線、モノレール3路線の計81路線が運行し、**高密度輸送**が行われています。JRだけでも、1日の乗車数は1600万人を超えます。複雑に入り組んだ過密なタイムスケジュールにもかかわらず、びっくりするほど正確に運行しています。地下鉄はメトロと呼ばれますが、清潔でスムーズできわめて優秀です。列車が3〜5分ごとに来るのに、どうしてドアが閉まろうとしている時に駆け込み乗車をする人がいるのかと思ってしまいます。もしも遅れが出ると、それがたとえ数分のことでも、**車掌**が繰り返し謝罪します。ラッシュアワー時の列車は通勤客がすし詰めです。席に座っている人の多くはぐっすりと睡眠しています。立っている人はたいていケータイでゲームをやっています。

　日本の高速列車は新幹線と呼ばれます。英語では「弾丸列車」と呼ばれることもあります。列車の先端の形が弾丸に似ているからです。新幹線は大都市から大都市に行くのにとても便利です。運行時間はきわめて正確で、発車、到着のいずれも1分1秒狂いがありません。日本のほとんどの地域で、新幹線は最高時速320キロで走ります。

52 交番 / コンビニ [koban / konbini]
Police Boxes / Convenience Stores

The *koban* system is a network of mini police stations that is unique to Japan. These "police boxes" can be found in almost every neighborhood. There are over 1,200 *koban* in Tokyo alone. They have a distinctive red light and a sign in alphabet saying KOBAN.

Not all of these stations are staffed 24 hours a day. In heavily populated cities, however, an officer will always be on duty. In popular tourist areas, there may be someone who can help tourists in English. People report thefts, lost articles, and traffic accidents at these small stations. Their most common service is to provide directions to businesses and tourist sights.

· · · · ·

Japan has more than 50,000 convenience stores. Traditionally convenience stores focused on selling beverages, cigarettes, snacks and other daily necessities. Most of their customers were males, but times have changed.

Recently, convenience stores are catering to new categories of customers. One group is *shinguru* or *ohitori-sama*, single people. With more households composed of single people, needs have changed. Convenience stores compete with large supermarkets by selling small portions of various products. You can buy a take-out boxed lunch and have it microwaved at the register. This is perfect for working women, elderly people and single men who do not have time or motivation to cook. (215words)

交番システムとはミニの警察署のネットワークで、日本独特のものです。こうした「ポリスボックス」はほとんどの地域にもあります。東京だけでも1200以上の交番があります。目印の赤いライトがあり、「KOBAN」とアルファベットで書かれています。

　すべての交番に、警官が **24時間体制** で常駐しているわけではありません。しかし、人口過密の街では、いつも **警官** が駐在しています。人気の観光地だと、観光客を英語で助けてくれる警官がいるかもしれません。交番には盗難、**遺失物**、交通事故などをとどけます。交番のもっともありふれた仕事は、会社や観光地に行く道を教えることです。

・・・・・

　日本には5万店以上のコンビニがあります。もともとコンビニで売っているのは、飲料、タバコ、スナック、その他**日用品**が中心でした。客のほとんどは男性でした。しかし時代は変わりました。

　最近のコンビニは新たな客層をターゲットにしています。一つは「シングル」もしくは「お一人様」、すなわち独身の人たちです。単身**世帯**が増えるにつれて、ニーズが変わってきました。コンビニは多様な商品を小分けして売ることで、大きなスーパーと競争しています。持ち帰りのお弁当を買って、レジのところの**電子レンジで温めてもらう**ことができます。働いている女性、高齢の人々、料理する時間もその気もない独身男性には、まさにぴったりです。

53 自動販売機 [jido hanbaiki]
Vending Machines

The country with the greatest total number of vending machines is the U.S., which has just less than 7 million, but Japan probably has more vending machines per person than any other country. An estimated 5 million machines sell cold drinks, hot drinks and the usual packaged snacks.

Japanese vending machines go way beyond that. They also dispense books, rental DVDs, umbrellas, written oracles (*omikuji*), noodles, ice cream, bananas, donuts, sliced pieces of apple, shaved ice, fresh eggs, *natto*, and packaged curry roux. A few of these machines sell bouquets of fresh flowers. A lingerie manufacturer has developed a bra-dispensing machine offering a range of colors. Attached are a size chart and samples to make choosing easy.

New high-tech vending machines have a touch-panel display. Products on the display change with the time of day. A sensor behind the panel estimates the user's age and gender, and personalizes its recommendations based on that assessment.

One new type of machine in sightseeing places offers free Wi-Fi. This is popular among foreign visitors who want to check email.

(176words)

| Round 1 | Round 2 | Round 3 | Round 4 | Round 5 | Round 6 |
| 月　　日 | 月　　日 | 月　　日 | 月　　日 | 月　　日 | 月　　日 |

　自動販売機の絶対数が一番多い国は7百万台弱のアメリカですが、日本は国民1人あたりの自動販売機の台数が世界一多い国です。推定5百万台の自動販売機があり、冷たい飲料、温かい飲料、おなじみのスナックのパックなどを売っています。

　しかし日本の自動販売機ははるか先まで進んでいます。本、レンタルDVD、傘、おみくじ、うどん、アイスクリーム、バナナ、ドーナッツ、むいたりんご、かき氷、生卵、納豆、カレールーのパックなども売っています。生花の**花束**を売る自動販売機まであります。下着メーカーは、色とりどりのブラジャーを売る自動販売機を開発しました。商品を選びやすいように、この機械にはサイズ表とサンプルがついています。

　新しいハイテクの自動販売機には、タッチパネルのディスプレイがついています。ディスプレイに出る商品は1日の時間の経過とともに変わります。パネルの後ろのセンサーが、お客の年齢と性別を判断します。この判断に基づき、お客に合わせておすすめ商品を決めます。

　無料でWiFiを提供する、新しいタイプの自動販売機が**観光地**にあります。メールをチェックしたい外国人観光客にとても人気です。

54 居酒屋 [izakaya]
Taverns

Izakaya are casual taverns, or drinking places. The atmosphere is relaxed and cheerful and the drinks and food are relatively inexpensive. *Izakaya* are sometimes called *akachochin*, "red lantern," because red paper lanterns are often used as advertisements outside such eateries.

Most customers begin by ordering a drink first and then looking at the menu. That drink is often referred to as *toriaezu biiru*, literally, "beer to start off with." A small appetizer, *otoshi*, is served with the drink as a kind of table charge. Diners order food and drink as they go. Unlike at other restaurants, customers share the dishes that are served. Typically customers have *edamame* (boiled and salted soybeans) or an assortment of *sashimi* first. Then they may have *yakitori* (grilled skewered chicken), grilled fish, tofu and maybe *ochazuke* at the end. When they are finished, they call for the bill and it will usually be brought to the table, but in most cases, they pay at the register as they leave the place.

Izakaya are used as places for "communication," especially among businesspeople on their way home from the office. Recently, however, among young people and sensible businesspeople, that view has increasingly come to be seen as nonsense. In any event, there can be no doubt that *izakaya* are a kind of holy place for older men who like to drink.

(233words)

| Round 1 | Round 2 | Round 3 | Round 4 | Round 5 | Round 6 |
| 月　　日 | 月　　日 | 月　　日 | 月　　日 | 月　　日 | 月　　日 |

　居酒屋は庶民的な酒場、つまり飲み屋です。リラックスした明るい雰囲気で、酒も食べ物も比較的安いです。居酒屋は赤ちょうちん、すなわち「赤いランタン」と呼ばれることもあります。なぜなら、赤いちょうちんが店の外に客引きのために飾ってあるからです。

　たいていの客はまず飲み物を注文し、その後でメニューを見ます。この飲み物は、「とりあえずビール」（文字通りには「まず最初にビール」という意味）と呼ばれることもあります。お通し（ちょっとした前菜）が、飲み物と一緒に出されますが、これはテーブルチャージのようなものです。飲み物と食べ物は、食事を進めながら注文していきます。他のレストランとは違って、客は出てきた料理を分け合って食べます。よくあるパターンとしては、まず枝豆（茹でて塩をふった大豆）か刺し身の盛り合わせを取ります。次に焼き鳥（串に刺したチキンを焼いたもの）、焼き魚、豆腐ときて、最後にお茶漬けを注文します。全部終わって、伝票をお願いしますと言うと、テーブルまでもってきてくれるのが普通です。ただし、勘定は帰るときに入り口近くのレジで払うことが多いです。

　居酒屋は、特にビジネスマンが仕事帰りに「コミュニケーションの一環」として利用します。ただ、最近は若い人や、割り切った考え方をするビジネスマンから、それはナンセンスだ、という意見が広まっています。いずれにしても、居酒屋が、お酒好きなおじさんの聖地であることは間違いありません。

55 銭湯 [sento]
Public Baths

Public baths (*sento*) originated in the Edo period, and men and women bathed together. The Meiji government banned mixed bathing, and gradually the sexes were divided. Sento are public bathhouses where baths are filled with heated water. When homes did not have bathing facilities, the residents of a community used the local public bath. Even though homes now have baths, some people still enjoy spending a leisurely time in a broad open bath.

Communal bathhouses have two entrances, one for women and one for men. Customers pay at the entrance and can stay as long as they want to. A tall barrier separates the sexes within one large changing room, where customers remove their clothing and put it in a locker. Bathers go into the bathing area, wash themselves with soap at individual faucets and then soak in a large bath. Some *sento* have a Jacuzzi-type bath, a mineral bath, or an additional lukewarm bath. Bathing at a *sento* is a great way to enjoy a unique Japanese experience without spending a lot of money.

(175words)

銭湯は江戸時代にはじまり、当時は男女混浴でした。男女混浴は明治政府によって禁止され、次第に男女の仕切りができるようになりました。銭湯は**公衆浴場**で、風呂には湯をはっています。各家庭に風呂の設備がなかったころ、地域の住民は地元の銭湯を利用しました。現在では各家庭に風呂がありますが、今でも、大きくて開放的な風呂でのんびりと過ごすのが好きな人もいます。

　銭湯には入り口が2つあります。女性用と男性用です。客は入り口でお金を払い、好きなだけ長くいることができます。脱衣場として1つの大きな部屋があり、高い仕切りによって男女が分けられています。ここで入浴客は衣服を脱ぎ、棚に入れます。ついで風呂場に入り、個別の**蛇口**の前で石けんで体を洗ってから、大きな湯船につかります。銭湯の中には、ぶくぶくと気泡の出る風呂、鉱泉の風呂、ぬるめの風呂がついている場合もあります。銭湯での入浴は、大金をかけずに日本独特の体験を満喫できる絶好の方法です。

56 天皇 [tenno]
The Emperor

The Emperor (*tenno*) is held to be a symbol of the unity of Japan and the Japanese people. This is stipulated in the Constitution of Japan. He plays no role in government administration. His duties are to carry out affairs of state at national ceremonies.

The founder of the imperial line is held to be Amaterasu Omikami, the guardian deity of the Imperial Household. Amaterasu Omikami is worshiped at shrines throughout the whole country. The head shrine is Ise Jingu.

The current *tenno* is Akihito. Members of the Imperial Family have a given name, but no surname. At the New Year, the Emperor greets the general public who gather in several sessions in the courtyard of the Imperial Palace. He carries out national ceremonies and receives foreign dignitaries on behalf of the country.

Since 2011 the Emperor and the Empress have repeatedly visited the areas devastated by the earthquake and tsunami in Tohoku. Public opinion favors these expressions of concern for ordinary citizens.

(161words)

天皇は、日本および日本国民統合の象徴とされています。それは、日本国憲法で規定されています。国政には関わりをもちません。国の儀式の際に、国事行為を行う義務があります。

　天皇の始祖は天照大神(あまてらすおおみかみ)とされ、皇室の氏神とされています。天照大神は全国各地の神社で祀られています。その総本社は伊勢神宮です。

　現在の天皇は昭仁です。天皇家には苗字がなく、名前しかありません。新年には天皇は、幾度かに分けて、皇居の中庭に集まる一般の人々に対してあいさつします。天皇は国家の儀式を執り行い、国の代表として外国の要人を迎えます。

　2011年以来、天皇と皇后は東北の地震と津波で被害を受けた地域を繰り返し訪問されています。このように一般市民への気遣いをお示しになることについて、世論は歓迎しています。

57 判子 [hanko]
Official and Private Seals

Official seals or stamps are engraved. They have the name of the organization or individual. They are pressed into a red inkpad (*shuniku*), then pressed on documents. In the West, people write their signature to show their agreement. In Japan, people stamp documents with one of two types of seals, either an official seal (*jitsuin*) or a private seal (*mitomein*).

For everyday purposes, most people use a simple, inexpensive seal (*hanko*). It is commonly called a *mitomein*. This is used when accepting a package delivery at home or at work to show that the person has seen and approved a memo.

Legal documents require an official seal (*jitsuin*). This is a specially engraved seal that has been registered at a local government office. The office issues a certificate proving that the seal is legally registered and can be used for contracts. This official seal makes documents legally binding. People may put their ordinary *hanko* in their pocket or in a desk drawer. But many people put their *jitsuin* in a safe place, so that no one will use it without their permission.

(183words)

Round 1	Round 2	Round 3	Round 4	Round 5	Round 6
月　　日	月　　日	月　　日	月　　日	月　　日	月　　日

　公印（つまり公のスタンプ）には文字が刻まれています。組織や個人の名前が記されています。朱肉に押し付けてから、文書に捺されます。西洋では同意を示すために署名を用いますが、日本では、実印と認印の2種類ある印のどちらかを文書に捺します。

　日常的な用途には、ほとんどの人は手軽で値のはらないはんこを用います。一般に認印と呼ばれます。家で宅配の荷物を受け取るときにも使います。仕事で、何か書類を見て承認したという意味で使うこともあります。

　法的文書には実印が必要です。実印というのは特注して彫ったはんこで、地元の役所に登録したものです。役所は、そのはんこが法的に登録済みのものであり、契約に使えるということを記した証明書を発行します。実印によって、文書が法的な拘束力をもったものとなります。ふつうの印鑑ならポケットに入れたり、デスクの引き出しに入れておいてもよいですが、実印はその人の許可なしに誰も使うことができないよう、安全な保管場所にしまっておくのがふつうです。

58 やくざ [yakuza]
Gangsters

Japanese gangsters (*yakuza*), are members of organized crime groups. Ironically, large yakuza organizations are officially registered with the police. Sometimes they are involved in right-wing politics. It is difficult to know how close they are to politicians who call for a return to the worship of the emperor and a stronger military.

The gangs are involved in blackmail, extortion, gambling, loan sharking, prostitution, and sales of stimulant drugs. They are also involved in the construction and entertainment industries.

Until recently, extensive tattoos were a symbol of belonging to one of these gangs. It was a symbol of their way of life as outlaws and it inspired fear. Now that tattoos are common among other groups, the power of that symbol has faded a bit.

The term "yakuza" is taken from a three-card game (*sanmai garuta*) that was popular during the Tokugawa period. It is like the card game blackjack. The count of the winning hand is closest to 19 but not over that number. Therefore *ya-ku-za* (8-9-3), which totals 20, is a losing hand in this game. One theory says gangsters adopted this term meaning "loser" as a way of rejecting the ideals of ordinary society.

(196words)

Round 1	Round 2	Round 3	Round 4	Round 5	Round 6
月　　日	月　　日	月　　日	月　　日	月　　日	月　　日

　ヤクザすなわち日本のギャングは犯罪組織に所属する者たちです。皮肉なことに、大きな暴力団組織は、正式に警察に登録されています。右翼の政治活動にからんでいる場合もあります。彼らが、天皇崇拝の復活や軍事力強化を叫ぶ政治家とどれくらい近いのか、ちょっと分かりかねるところがあります。

　暴力団が行うのは恐喝、ゆすり、ギャンブル、高利貸し、売春、覚せい剤の販売などです。土建業、娯楽産業にもからんでいます。

　最近まで、大きな刺青がこうした暴力団に属しているシンボルでした。アウトローとしての生き方を象徴するもので、人の恐怖心をそそるものでした。現在では刺青が他の集団のあいだでもふつうになってきているので、このシンボルとしての威力は多少弱まっています。

「やくざ」という語は、徳川時代に流行した三枚がるたというゲームから来ています。このゲームは、トランプのブラックジャックというゲームに似ています。あがり札の合計が 19 に一番近いものが勝ちですが、19 を越えてはいけません。したがって、やくざ（8、9、3）だと合計 20 となり、このゲームでは負けです。一説には、かたぎ社会の理想を拒否するために、「負け札」を意味するこの語を使い始めたのだといいます。

59 入学試験 [nyugaku shiken]
Entrance Examinations

Entrance examinations (*nyugaku shiken*) are very important in the educational system of Japan. There are exams to enter each level of schooling, from private primary school to university. The most important exams are those for entering university. Students go to after-school *juku* (private tutoring academies) or *yobiko* (cram schools) to get into high-level universities.

Each university has its own exams, usually in February and March, for entrance to school on the 1st of April. Because national universities are inexpensive and prestigious, the competition to enter is fierce. The exams may include an objective achievement test, an essay-writing test, and perhaps an interview. The exams do not have a minimum score that guarantees admission. The test scores simply line up the candidates from top to bottom for a limited number of openings.

Applicants who fail to enter their desired university may take an extra year to study. They are called *ronin*, after the masterless samurai of the Edo period. The *ronin* devote another year to preparing for another once-a-year exam.

The university a student gets into influences his or her destiny. Graduating from a well-known university opens the door to well-known companies at hiring time. Some companies hire only from prestigious universities.

(200words)

Round 1	Round 2	Round 3	Round 4	Round 5	Round 6
月　　日	月　　日	月　　日	月　　日	月　　日	月　　日

　入学試験は日本の教育システムの中できわめて重要です。**私立小学校**から大学まで、どの段階の教育機関に入るにも試験があります。もっとも重要な試験は大学に入学するための試験です。よい大学に入るため、高校生は塾（個人指導のための私的な学校)や**予備校**に学校が終わってから行きます。

　４月１日入学のため、大学はそれぞれ２月か３月に独自に試験を行います。国立大学は学費が安く聞こえもよいので、入学するには熾烈な競争があります。試験は客観的な学力テスト、論文試験などで、**面接**のある場合もあります。入学を保証する最低点があるわけではありません。受験生は単純にテストの結果で上から下まで順に並べられ、限られた枠を競うわけです。

　希望の大学に入学できなかった受験生は、もう１年勉強するかもしれません。浪人と呼ばれますが、この語は、江戸時代の主人のいない侍からきています。浪人は、１年に１度の試験をもう１度受ける準備をするために、もう１年ささげるのです。

　どんな大学に入るかで、その人の運命が決まります。有名大学を卒業すれば、就職のときに有名企業に入れる可能性があります。名の通った大学からしか採用しない企業もあります。

60 ヤンキー / カラオケ [yankii / karaoke]

Delinquents / Karaoke

Yankii sounds like it comes from the English word "yankee," but the two are not related in meaning. The *yankii* subculture appeared in the media in the 1980s and 1990s. The word referred to young men and women who wore rebellious clothes. They were famous for being loud and rude, and refused to follow the strict rules of Japanese culture. They were basically a type of delinquent students. They dyed their hair and wore it in pompadours. They shaved their eyebrows to make themselves look frightening. Perhaps the closest thing in the West were the punks.

Their attitude usually involved being poor students, having poor manners, and causing trouble. After graduating from high school, most took lower-paid jobs to make ends meet.

・ ・ ・ ・ ・

The Japanese word *karaoke* comes from *kara*, meaning "empty," and *oke*, the first syllables of "orchestra" (*okesutora*). It means musical accompaniment without the singing portion. Karaoke is prerecorded musical accompaniment for singing at home, in bars, and rent-by-the-hour studios (*karaoke-bokkusu*). The word also refers to a place that provides this kind of music.

Karaoke establishments offer individual soundproof rooms for individuals and small groups. The patrons select a song. Then they sing along to the lyrics that appear on a video monitor.

(203words)

「ヤンキー」という音だけ聞くと、英語の「ヤンキー」がもとになっているように感じられます。しかし、意味的には英語の「ヤンキー」とは関係がありません。「ヤンキー」のサブカルチャーは1980年代、1990年代にマスコミに取り上げられました。ヤンキーとは、反抗的な服を着ている少年少女のことです。声がでかい、傍若無人だということで有名でした。彼らは日本文化の厳しい決まりに従うことを拒否しました。基本的には不良高校生の1タイプです。髪を染め、リーゼントにしました。まゆを剃って、威嚇的に見えるようにしました。おそらく、西洋でこれに一番近いのは**パンク**でしょう。

　ヤンキーになると、落ちこぼれ、礼儀知らず、トラブルを起こすなどの行動につながるのがふつうでした。彼らはたいてい高校を卒業すると生活のために低賃金の仕事につきました。

・・・・・

　日本語の「カラオケ」は、「空っぽ」という意味の「カラ」と、「オーケストラ」の最初の2文字である「オケ」からできています。伴奏だけあって、歌の部分のないものを意味します。カラオケは、家やバーやカラオケボックス（**時間貸し**のスタジオ）で歌うために、音楽の伴奏だけがあらかじめ録音されたものです。このような音楽を提供する店を指すこともあります。

　カラオケの店は、個人や小さなグループ客のために、個別の**防音室**を提供します。客が歌を選ぶと、ビデオのモニターに**歌詞**が出てくるので、それにしたがって歌います。

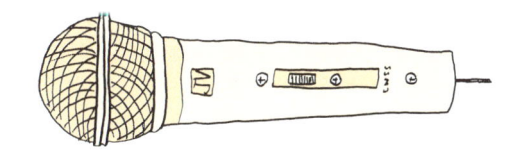

61 アイドル/オタク [aidoru/otaku]
Idols / Otaku

An *aidoru*, from the English word "idol," is an innocent young woman who is either beautiful or has some distinctive feature. A girl can become famous most often by appearing in magazines in skimpy bathing suits. If she can sing (or even if she can't), she may get a chance to appear on a music show on television. If she has a unique personality, she may appear on a talk show, just looking cute.

These "idols" are created by production companies, who recruit and groom these performers. Some girls are super sweet; some appear to have no personality. They do not need to be talented; being average is okay. They just need to capture some kind of audience who will buy their CDs and photo albums.

・・・・・

An *otaku*, a geek, is someone who spends a lot of spare time cultivating interests in video games, manga, anime or even just the Internet. In the 1990s, the word had a negative nuance. It implied that the person had no social life outside of these hobbies. Nowadays, *otaku* means someone who is a fan of some part of Japanese culture. The word is used overseas as well. The term *otaku* is used for people who are excessively interested in manga, anime, figurines, computers, trains, robots or girl groups.

(215words)

Round 1	Round 2	Round 3	Round 4	Round 5	Round 6
月　　日	月　　日	月　　日	月　　日	月　　日	月　　日

「アイドル」という語は英語の"idol"からできた言葉ですが、美少女であるか、もしくは何かユニークなところのある無垢な女の子のことを指します。女の子は布を節約した水着で雑誌にのると、有名になるというパターンがとても多いです。歌が歌えれば（または、歌が歌えなくとも）、テレビの音楽番組に出るという手もあります。**人と違った個性**があれば、バラエティに出してもらえるかもしれません。かわいい顔をして座っているだけですが。

　このようなアイドルは芸能プロダクションによって作り出されます。会社がこうしたタレントをスカウトして、仕込むのです。超かわいい少女もいれば、何の特徴もないような少女もいます。才能がないとだめというわけではありません。ごくふつうで大丈夫です。ある種のファンの心をつかんで、CDや写真集を買って貰えればそれでよいのです。

・・・・・

オタク（変わり者 geek）というのは、テレビゲーム、漫画、アニメ、もしくは、ただインターネットにはまり込んで長時間すごす人のことです。1990年代には、この語はマイナスイメージを持っていました。こうした趣味以外では社会生活を持たない人、というニュアンスでした。今では、オタクは、日本文化の中の何かある分野のファンである人、という意味です。この語は海外でも使われます。オタクとは、漫画、アニメ、**フィギュア**、コンピュータ、鉄道、ロボット、少女のアイドルグループなどに過剰に入れこんでいる人のことです。

(*´∀`)♪

62 お正月 / 駅伝 [oshogatsu / ekiden]
Japanese New Year / Long-distance Relay Race

Oshogatsu is the first several days of the New Year. New Year's Day is called *gantan*. During the period of *Oshogatsu*, many Japanese pay a visit to a shrine or temple, which is called *hatsumode*.

Hatsumode is the first visit to a Shinto shrine or a Buddhist temple in the New Year. Visitors go to pray for health and happiness in the New Year. Visitors may draw "sacred lots" (*omikuji*), which evaluate the person's luck in several categories for the coming year. Visitors may also buy good luck charms, such as *ofuda*, which are supposed to protect a house and those who live in it.

・・・・・

The Japanese word *ekiden* combines the character *eki* (station) and *den* (relay). An *ekiden* is a team relay race. Each participant runs from one "station" to the next. The runner then passes on a cloth sash (*tasuki*) to the next runner on the team.

The most popular *ekiden* in Japan is the two-day Hakone *Ekiden* for college men on January 2 and 3 during New Year. It is a competition between Japanese universities that draws a lot of attention. Each team has ten runners who cover the round-trip between Tokyo and Hakone, a total of 219 kilometers.

The entire race is broadcast live on national television and has a high audience rating. Crowds of a million or more line the route to cheer on the runners.

(233words)

Round 1	Round 2	Round 3	Round 4	Round 5	Round 6
月　　日	月　　日	月　　日	月　　日	月　　日	月　　日

「お正月」というのは新年の最初の数日のことです。1月1日は「元旦」と呼ばれます。お正月のあいだに、多くの日本人は神社かお寺にお参りします。これは「初詣」と呼ばれます。

初詣というのは、新年になって初めて神社やお寺に参詣することです。新年の健康と幸せを祈願するために行きます。おみくじを引く人もいるでしょう。おみくじは、いくつかの項目について、その人の来る年の運勢を予言してくれます。御札など幸運のお守りを買う人もいるでしょう。御札は、家屋やそこに住んでいる家族を守ってくれるものとされています。

・・・・・

日本語の「駅伝」という語は、「駅（ステーション）」と「伝（リレー）」という文字が組み合わさったものです。駅伝というのはチームによるリレーレースです。選手はそれぞれひとつの「駅」から次の「駅」まで走ります。ランナーは次の駅でチームの次の走者にたすきを渡します。

日本でもっとも人気の駅伝は、男子大学生が出る、1月2日、3日の2日間に渡って行われる箱根駅伝です。日本の大学どうしの競い合いで、大きな注目を集めます。10人のランナーが、東京―箱根間を往復して合計219キロを走ります。

レース全体が全国ネットでテレビ放映され、高い視聴率を得ています。100万人以上の人が沿道に並んで、選手に声援をおくります。

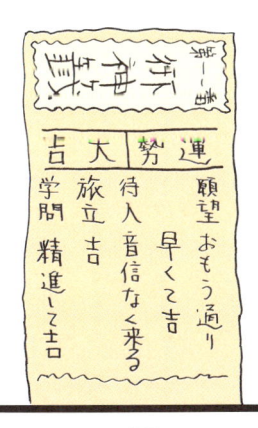

このページに、使ってみたい英語表現や、覚えておきたい英単語などを書き込んでおきましょう

Chapter 6
海外の方に人気の観光地ベスト10

63 伊勢神宮・出雲大社
[ise jingu / izumo taisha]
Ise Grand Shrine & Izumo Taisha Grand Shrine

Ise Grand Shrine (*Ise Jingu*), in Mie Prefecture, is the most important Shinto shrine in the country. It enshrines Amaterasu, the Sun Goddess, who is represented by a sacred mirror. The mirror is considered one of the three sacred regalia (*sanshu no jingi*). The Outer Shrine (*Geku*), enshrines Toyouke no Omikami, the god of food and agriculture. Each of the main shrine buildings is rebuilt every twenty years on an adjacent lot. The old shrine is taken down and the space is left open. This regular rebuilding is part of a belief in the renewal of nature.

Izumo Taisha Grand Shrine (*Izumo Taisha*) in Shimane Prefecture is another ancient and important shrine. It enshrines Okuninushi-no-Okami, a deity of agriculture, marriage and good fortune. The current shrine is 24 meters high but archaeologists believe that the ancient shrine was almost 96 meters high. In ancient times, people believed that all of the *kami* from around the country gathered at Izumo in October. These deities went there to confer about their local regions. Today the shrine is popular for bringing men and women together in marriage (*enmusubi*).

(188words)

| Round 1 | Round 2 | Round 3 | Round 4 | Round 5 | Round 6 |
| 月　　日 | 月　　日 | 月　　日 | 月　　日 | 月　　日 | 月　　日 |

　伊勢神宮は三重県にありますが、日本で最も格の高い神社です。内宮には天 照 大 神（太陽の女神）をお祀りしています。ご神体は神聖な鏡です。鏡は**三種の神器**の１つとされています。外宮には豊 受 大神がお祀りされています。食べ物と穀物の神様です。20 年ごとに、主要な正殿、社殿はすべて隣接地に建て替えられます。古い建物は取り壊され、跡地は空き地のまま置かれます。この定期的な建て替えは、自然の再生への信仰を表したものです。

　島根県の出雲大社も、由緒ある格の高い神社です。この神社にお祀りされているのは大国 主 大神で、五穀豊穣、縁結び、幸運の神様です。現在の本殿は高さ 24 メートルですが、考古学者によれば、古代にはおよそ 96 メートルであったと言われています。古代には、国中の神が 10 月に出雲に集まると信じられていました。それぞれの地域について話すために集まったのです。今日では出雲大社は縁結び、すなわち男女を結びつけてくれるということで人気があります。

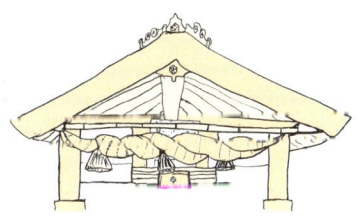

64 日光東照宮 [nikko toshogu]
Nikko Toshogu

Nikko was a sacred mountain for ascetics beginning in the Nara period. It is the site of Toshogu, the mausoleum of Tokugawa Ieyasu, the founder of the Tokugawa shogunate. It was built in Nikko according to his will. He wanted to be enshrined there as *Tosho-dai-gongen*, "a deity who shines and protects the east."

Originally, the shrine was small. Iemitsu, his grandson, decided to build an elegantly decorated shrine to commemorate the long-lasting peace that Ieyasu had created. It is now a major attraction.

At the approach to the shrine gate is a stable for sacred horses. One of the panels under the roof is carved with three monkeys (*sanzaru*) which teaches the wisdom "see no evil, hear no evil, speak no evil." The *Yomei-mon* is the most famous structure at Toshogu. This gate is elaborately carved and multicolored. Inside is another gate called *Kara-mon*. The main shrine is an important space where the worlds of gods and humans connect.

Toshogu mixes Shinto with Buddhism. The main hall is a Shinto shrine, but the pagoda is Buddhist. There is also a Buddhist sutra storehouse. The chief figure in the construction of Toshogu was a Buddhist monk named Tenkai, but he chose to declare Ieyasu a Shinto god instead of a Buddha.

(211words)

Round 1	Round 2	Round 3	Round 4	Round 5	Round 6
月　日	月　日	月　日	月　日	月　日	月　日

　日光は奈良時代以降、**修験者**のための神聖な山でした。ここには東照宮、すなわち徳川幕府を開いた徳川家康の**霊廟**があります。日光に建立されたのは家康の**遺言**によるものです。東照大権現、すなわち東国を照らし守護する神として祀られることを望んだのです。

　最初この神社は小さかったのですが、家康の**孫**の家光が、家康によって築き上げられた**長い平和の時代**を記念するために、瀟洒な装飾の施された神社を建立することにしたのです。現在では観光の目玉になっています。

　神社の門にいたる参道には、神馬のための**厩**があります。この厩の屋根の下の長押の1枚に、3匹の猿（三猿）が彫刻されています。この3匹は「**見ざる、聞かざる、言わざる**」という知恵を教えています。東照宮でもっとも有名な建築物は陽明門です。この門には凝った彫刻が施され、きらびやかな彩色がなされています。その内側にはもうひとつ唐門と呼ばれる門があります。本殿は神々の世界と人間の世界が結びつく重要な空間です。

　東照宮では神道と仏教が習合しています。**本殿**は神道です。塔は仏教のものです。仏教の**経典**を収める建物もあります。東照宮の建立に際して中心となったのは天海という仏僧でしたが、家康を仏教ではなく神道の神にすることにしたのです。

65 築地 [tsukiji]
Tsukiji Market

Tokyo's major fish market was moved to Tsukiji in the mid-1920s and the current market was completed in 1935. Tsukiji is located between the upscale Ginza shopping area and the Sumida River. It is now the Tokyo Metropolitan Central Wholesale Market, which handles seafood, fruit and vegetables. When someone mentions Tsukiji, most people think of fish, but it is also one of the largest wholesale food markets of any kind. In the inner wholesale market (*jonai-shijo*) some 900 licensed wholesale dealers sell, buy and process fish. Visitors are only allowed in limited areas.

Tons of frozen tuna and other fish begin to arrive when the market opens at 3:00 a.m. The tuna auction in the market starts in the early morning. Overseas visitors, in restricted numbers, are allowed to view from special viewing areas.

The outer retail market (*jogai-shijo*) sells fruit, vegetables, food products, and restaurant supplies. Its many restaurants, especially sushi shops, attract local customers and domestic and overseas visitors. This market closes in the early afternoon.

The Tokyo Metropolitan Government will move the wholesale market to Toyosu, further east from Tsukiji. The retail market will be remodeled on the present site.

(193words)

Round 1	Round 2	Round 3	Round 4	Round 5	Round 6
月　　日	月　　日	月　　日	月　　日	月　　日	月　　日

　1920年代の中頃、東京の代表的な**魚市場**が築地に移され、1935年に現在のマーケットが完成しました。築地は銀座の高級なショッピング街と隅田川の間に位置しています。現在では東京都中央卸売市場となり、海産物、果物、野菜を扱っています。築地と言えば魚のイメージですが、どんな種類の食品についても世界最大級の**卸売食品市場**になっています。場内市場（中の卸売市場）では、認可を受けた900ほどの業者が魚を売り、買い、さばいています。観光客が立ち入りを許されているのは**限られた区域**だけです。

　午前3時にマーケットが開くと、冷凍マグロをはじめとする何トンもの魚が到着しはじめます。マグロの競りは早朝に始まります。人数に制限がありますが、海外の観光客は場内を特別の見学区域から見ることができます。

　場外市場（外の**小売市場**）では野菜や果物、加工食品、レストラン用の食材などを売っています。寿司屋などたくさんのレストランがあり、地元の客、国内の旅行者、海外の観光客が利用しています。場外市場は昼過ぎに終了となります。

　東京都は卸売市場を、築地より東の豊洲に移転する計画です。小売市場は現在の場所で再開発されることになります。

66 浅草寺 [sensoji]
Sensoji (Asakusa Kannon)

Sensoji is the oldest temple in Tokyo. It dates from 628, when two fishermen are said to have found a small gold image of the Boddhisattva Kannon in their fishing net. The local people built a small temple for the statue near the Sumida River. Since that time, the temple has been destroyed and rebuilt many times. The current building was completed in 1958.

The main gate of the temple houses the God of Wind (Fujin) and the God of Thunder (Raijin). These gods are believed to protect against fire and natural disasters. They are also believed to bring large harvests. The gate is called Kaminari-mon, literally "Thunder Gate." The gate is also famous for its enormous red paper lantern (*chochin*). Between this gate and the temple is a long street called Nakamise-dori. Shops along both sides of this street sell souvenirs of varying quality, *sembei* (rice crackers), traditional sweets, woodblock prints, *tenugui* (printed towels), T-shirts, mobile phone straps, ceramic ware, and miniature figures based on traditional themes. Sensoji is one of the most popular places for *hatsumode* in the Tokyo area.

(182words)

| Round 1 | Round 2 | Round 3 | Round 4 | Round 5 | Round 6 |
| 月　　日 | 月　　日 | 月　　日 | 月　　日 | 月　　日 | 月　　日 |

　浅草寺は東京でもっとも古い寺です。その歴史は628年にまでさかのぼります。小さな黄金の観音菩薩像が網にかかっているのを、2人の漁師が見つけました。土地の人々がこの像のために、隅田川近くに小さなお寺を建立しました。それ以来、このお寺は幾度となく破壊されては再建されてきました。現在の建物が完成したのは1958年のことです。

　このお寺の表門には、風神像と雷神像が蔵されています。これらの神は火事や自然の災害から守ってくれると信じられています。また、豊作をもたらしてくれるとも考えられています。この門は雷門と呼ばれます（文字通りには「雷の門」です）。この門は、巨大な赤い紙の提灯でも有名です。この門とお寺の間には、仲見世通りと呼ばれる長い通りがあります。この通りの両側に店がずらりと並んでいて、おみやげを売っています。せんべい（ライスクラッカー）、昔ながらのお菓子、木版画、手ぬぐい（絵を染めたタオル）、Tシャツ、ケータイのストラップ、陶器、昔話をネタにしたミニチュア人形など、上等のものから安めのものまでピンからキリです。浅草寺は初詣の場所として、東京方面で最も人気のある場所の1つです。

67 銀座 [ginza] / Ginza

The name Ginza, literally "silver mint," refers to the mints for casting silver coins that were built in the early 17th century by the Tokugawa shogunate.

In the early Meiji period, it became a center of Western fashion and culture. South of it is Shimbashi, the terminal of the early train line that was built to Yokohama. East of it is Tsukiji, which at that time was the residence of many foreigners and the location of several new universities. Following a fire that destroyed most of the area in 1872, the government designated Ginza as an area for the construction of fireproof brick structures. Eventually it flourished as a place to shop, be seen, and look at fashion.

Today, Ginza is one of the most upscale shopping districts in the world. Its center is Ginza-Dori, which is closed to vehicle traffic on weekends and holidays (*hokosha tengoku*). Department stores and expensive boutiques line both sides of the street. Along the back streets are art galleries, coffee shops, restaurants and bars. When night falls, expensive clubs open their doors.

East of this main street are the famous Kabukiza theater and the Tsukiji market.

(196words)

銀座は文字通りには「**銀貨製造所**」ということで、17世紀初頭に徳川幕府によって建てられた銀貨の鋳造所のことを指しています。

　明治初頭には、西洋のファッションと文化の中心地となりました。南には新橋駅、すなわち横浜まで作られた初期の鉄道の**終着駅**がありました。東側は築地ですが、その当時の築地には多くの外国人が居住し、何校か新しい大学がありました。1872年に大火があり、この地域の大半を焼きつくしたので、それを受けて政府は、銀座を耐火性の高いレンガ造りの建物を建てる地域に指定しました。最終的に銀座は、ショッピングし、おしゃれをし、ファッションを見に行く場所として栄えました。

　今日では、銀座は世界で有数の**高級ショッピング街**となっています。中心は銀座通りで、週末や祝祭日には歩行者天国になっています。通りの両側に、デパートや高級ブティックが軒を並べています。裏通りには画廊、コーヒー店、レストラン、バーなどがあります。暗くなると、値段の高いクラブがドアを開けます。

　この大通りの東には有名な歌舞伎座と築地市場があります。

東北 [tohoku]
Tohoku (Northeast Honshu)

Northeast Honshu, called Tohoku, is largely mountainous. It is primarily an agricultural area with rice, cherries (*sakuranbo*), and apples among its notable crops. Forestry and fishing are also important.

Sendai, the principal city, was formerly the castle town of Date Masamune, one of the strongest *daimyo*. Masamune built Aoba Castle on a hill overlooking the Hirose River and the broad plain beyond.

Near Sendai is Matsushima Bay, which has some 260 tiny scenic pine-covered islands. The 17th-century haiku poet Matsuo Basho celebrated the beautiful sight in a poem in his 1694 travel diary *The Narrow Road to the Deep North* (*Oku no Hosomichi*).

Further north is Hiraizumi, now a World Heritage Site. It is known for its temples, gardens and the Konjikido, the Golden Hall. Hiraizumi was home of three generations of Fujiwara lords who hoped to build a peaceful domain to compete with Kyoto. Basho composed a haiku of great pathos here when he saw how those dreams were dashed and how little was left.

Tohoku is now also well known for the unfortunate events that happened there on March 11, 2011. Its Pacific coastline was devastated by an enormous earthquake that generated recurrent tsunami. On top of that, the Fukushima Nuclear Power Plant that suffered damage experienced a meltdown second only to Chernobyl.

(192 words)

Round 1	Round 2	Round 3	Round 4	Round 5	Round 6
月　　日	月　　日	月　　日	月　　日	月　　日	月　　日

　本州の北東部、すなわち東北は大部分が山です。基本的に農業地帯で、主要農産物として、米、さくらんぼ、りんごなどが挙げられます。林業、漁業も重要産業です。

　東北の中心都市である仙台は、かつて伊達政宗の城下町でした。伊達政宗は有力大名の一人です。広瀬川とその先の広々とした平野を見下ろす丘の上に、政宗は青葉城を建てました。

　仙台の近くに松島湾があります。この湾には260ほどの、まさに絵に描いたような松の木の茂る小島が浮かんでいます。この美しい風景を、17世紀の俳人松尾芭蕉は、1694年の紀行文『奥の細道』で俳句にうたっています。

　北に行くと平泉があります。現在では世界遺産となっています。お寺、庭園、金色堂が有名です。平泉は藤原三代の本拠地でした。彼らは京都と肩を並べる、平和な国を築こうとしました。芭蕉はそうした夢がはかなく潰えて、跡にほとんど何も残っていないのを見て、深い哀調をおびた俳句を詠みました。

　東北は2011年の3月11日、残念なことで有名になりました。巨大地震と、それによって生じた数次の津波によって、太平洋岸が壊滅的打撃を受けたのです。そればかりか、損傷した原子力発電所がチェルノブイリにつぐひどいメルトダウンを経験したのです。

69 原宿・明治神宮 [*harajuku / meiji jingu*]
Harajuku & Meiji Shrine

file-69

Harajuku Station on the Yamanote Line is the entrance to two worlds. On one side of the tracks is the quiet Meiji Shrine. On the other side are Omotesando Boulevard and Takeshita Dori. Omotesando has upscale boutiques, pricey foreign brand stores, and the character-goods heaven, Kiddy Land. It is a great place to watch people in their most fashionable outfits. To one side of this boulevard is Takeshita Dori, a magnet for young people. Clothing stores sell Gothic Lolita and *visual-kei* clothes, collectors' items and accessories. Prices are generally low and the road is packed with visitors.

Ironically, the bridge connecting Harajuku Station with the Meiji Shrine is a gathering place for cosplayers. Some imitate *anime* characters and others create their own unique attire. Arriving on Sunday in the late morning, their outrageous styles attract a large audience of photographers.

The Meiji Shrine (*Meiji Jingu*), honors the spirit of Emperor Meiji. During his reign, the country underwent modernization. Although the shrine is not exceptionally beautiful, it is surrounded by an impressive wooded park. The main shrine and *torii* gate were rebuilt in 1958. Next to it is Yoyogi Park, where many people come to picnic on weekends.

(197words)

Round 1	Round 2	Round 3	Round 4	Round 5	Round 6
月　　日	月　　日	月　　日	月　　日	月　　日	月　　日

　山手線の原宿駅は２つの世界への入り口になっています。線路の片側は静かな明治神宮です。反対側には表参道の**大通り**と竹下通りがあります。表参道は高級ブティック、高価な外国のブランド店、キャラクター商品の天国であるキディランドなどの中心です。最先端のファッションをまとった人たちを見るには絶好の場所です。大通りの片側に竹下通りがあります。若い人たちが集まる場所です。ありとあらゆる種類の洋品店があり、ゴスロリやヴィジュアル系の服、コレクター用の品物、アクセサリーなどを売っています。値段は概して安く、道には客があふれています。

　皮肉なことに、原宿駅と明治神宮を結ぶ陸橋はコスプレ愛好者の溜まり場になっています。アニメのキャラクターを真似ている人も入れば、独自の衣装を自分で創っている人もいます。日曜の朝遅くなってから行ってみると、こうした人たちの奇妙奇天烈な格好に、たくさんのカメラマンが吸い寄せられています。

　明治神宮は明治天皇の御魂をお祀りしているところです。明治天皇の御代に、日本は**近代化**を経験しました。この神社はよそと比べて格別に美しいというわけではありませんが、社を取り巻く森の公園がとてもみごとです。本殿と鳥居は 1958 年に再建されました。隣は代々木公園になっていて、週末には大勢の人がやってきてピクニックを楽しみます。

70 富士山 [fuji-san]
Mt. Fuji

The beautiful slopes of Mt. Fuji were created by smooth flows of lava from the caldera at the top. The most recent eruption of this active volcano was in 1707. Ash from this eruption drifted as far as Edo (now Tokyo), covering the city.

These slopes are clearly visible because there are no other mountains around it to block the view. During the winter, when the atmosphere is clearer, the mountain can even be seen from many high points in central Tokyo.

Mountain worshippers began climbing Mt. Fuji in the Heian period as a religious rite. The mountain itself was considered a *kami* or deity. During the Edo period, religious groups called *Fuji-ko* organized pilgrimages, which encouraged more and more ordinary people to make the climb. But as late as the Meiji period, women were not allowed to climb to the upper stations along the climbing route.

Fuji-san is a UNESCO World Heritage Site. The base of the mountain is easily accessible by car or train. The official climbing season is July and August. During the off-season, the huts at the summit are closed. It is a strenuous climb and requires training and proper equipment, even during the official climbing season.

(201words)

Round 1	Round 2	Round 3	Round 4	Round 5	Round 6
月　　日	月　　日	月　　日	月　　日	月　　日	月　　日

　富士山の美しい曲線は、山頂のカルデラから溶岩がなめらかに流れ出ることによって創り出されたものです。この活火山が最後に噴火したのは1707年のことです。この噴火で出た火山灰は江戸（現在の東京）にまで吹き流されて、江戸の町全体を覆いました。

　山の曲線は、視界をさえぎる山が周りにないのではっきりと見えます。冬には空気がきれいなので、富士山は東京の中心の高い場所からでも見えます。

　山岳信仰により、人々は平安時代に行(ぎょう)として富士山に登りはじめました。富士山そのものが神であると考えられていました。江戸時代には富士講と呼ばれる宗教団体が団体旅行を組織し、そのおかげで、富士山に登る一般の人がどんどん増えていきました。しかしなんと明治時代になるまで、登山道の上の方は女人禁制でした。

　富士山はユネスコの世界文化遺産です。山裾までは自動車でも鉄道でも簡単に行けます。正式な登山シーズンは7、8月です。シーズンオフには山頂の山小屋は閉鎖されます。きつい登山なので、正式な登山シーズンでも訓練と適切な装備は欠かせません。

71 秋葉原 [akihabara]
Akihabara

The name Akihabara comes from the name of the Akiba Shrine, built there in the late 19th century. After World War II, the area flourished as a black market with street stalls selling vacuum tubes and radios.

Partly because it is a major public transportation hub, it now flourishes as a center for electrical appliances and electronic goods. Hundreds of wholesale and retail stores, small and gigantic, draw enormous crowds.

Akihabara has also become a center of *otaku* culture. Many stores deal in *manga*-related goods. The Gundam Café, for example, features décor and menu items based on the popular robot animated TV series. Plastic-modeling company Kaiyodo's "Hobby Lobby Tokyo" specializes in high-quality models of unique subjects. These include Tokyo landmark models (such as Asakusa's Kaminari-mon) and poseable Buddhist action figures. Other attractions are entertainment cafés with various themes. "Maid cafés" feature costumed waitresses, some who look like "idols" and some who dress like manga characters. Interaction between the waitresses and customers is part of the experience. The phenomenally successful idol group AKB48 has its own AKB48 Café and Shop, which has its own standing-room only theater.

(185words)

Round 1	Round 2	Round 3	Round 4	Round 5	Round 6
月　　日	月　　日	月　　日	月　　日	月　　日	月　　日

　秋葉原という地名は、19世紀末に建立された秋葉神社の名に由来します。第2次世界大戦のあと、この地域は、露天の店で**真空管**やラジオを売っている闇市で栄えました。

　公共交通機関の重要な**乗換駅**となっているということもあり、現在では電気器具や電気製品の販売の中心地として繁栄しています。卸と小売の大小含めて数百もの店に、ものすごい数の人々が吸い寄せられてきます。

　加えて、秋葉原はオタク文化の中心地にもなっています。漫画関連商品を売っている店が多くあります。例えばガンダムカフェは、ロボットの人気アニメのテレビシリーズに基づいた**内装**とメニューが売り物です。プラモデルの会社、海洋堂の「ホビーロビー東京」は、ユニークなテーマの高級プラモデルを扱っています。その中には東京の名所モデル（例えば浅草の雷門など）、幅広いアクションポーズを取らせることができる仏像、などがあります。その他人気の場所として、様々なテーマに基づく遊びカフェがあります。「メイドカフェ」はメイドの衣装を着たウェイトレスが売り物で、アイドルのような顔の女の子も、漫画のキャラクターに扮した女の子もいます。ウェイトレスと客の**やりとり**も楽しみの一部です。大ヒットしたアイドルグループAKB48は、「AKB48カフェ＆ショップ」を独自に持っていて、そこには**立ち見だけの劇場**があります。

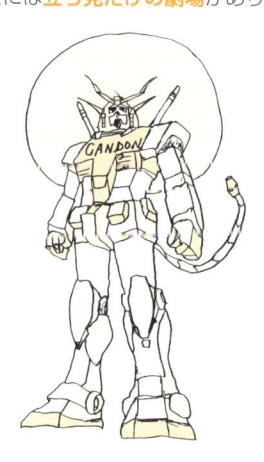

72 京都・奈良 [kyoto/nara]
Kyoto & Nara Page 1

Nara was the imperial capital from 710 to 784. During those years, Buddhism became the religion of the court and the nation. Near Nara, the Buddhist temple Horyuji was originally built around 711, but later burned down. Nonetheless, the current structure is the oldest wooden building in the world. In the center of Nara, Todaiji houses a 15-meter-high Vairocana Buddha, the largest bronze Buddha statue in the world. Nearby Nigatsu-do, "Second-Month Hall," is famous for its annual *Omizu-tori* (drawing of sacred water), ceremony held at night. Kasuga Grand Shrine is famous for its stone lanterns and hanging lanterns.

Kyoto, capital for a millennium, may be the best sightseeing city in the world. Many parts of the city were burned down in the Onin War (1467-77), but the city was spared from the air raids of World War II. The city has more than 20% of Japan's National Treasures and the following are just a few highlights.

Kinkakuji, the three-story Golden Pavilion, was destroyed by arson in 1950, but the exact replica built in 1955 is stunning. It is covered with gold leaf applied with *urushi*, Japanese lacquer. Ginkakuji, the Silver Pavilion, built in 1482, is famous for its garden. It was the center of culture flourishing in the eastern mountains of the capital. Ryoanji, a Zen temple, encloses the famous rock garden, which is considered a visual representation of Zen teachings.

| Round 1 | Round 2 | Round 3 | Round 4 | Round 5 | Round 6 |
| 月　　日 | 月　　日 | 月　　日 | 月　　日 | 月　　日 | 月　　日 |

　奈良は 710 年から 784 年まで**帝都**でした。この間に仏教が**宮廷**及び国の宗教となりました。奈良の近くにある仏教寺の法隆寺は、最初は 711 年頃に建立されましたが後に焼失しました。とはいえ、現在の建物は**世界最古の木造建築**です。奈良の中心に東大寺があり、高さ 15 メートルの盧遮那仏が蔵されています。このブロンズ製の仏像は世界で最大です。その近くの二月堂は年中行事であるお水取りで有名です。お水取りというのは神聖な水を汲む儀式で、夜に行われます。春日大社は石燈籠と**釣燈籠**が有名です。

　京都は千年の都で、世界中でもっともすばらしい**観光都市**でしょう。京都の多くの部分が応仁の乱（1467 〜 77）で焼け落ちましたが、第 2 次世界大戦中の**空襲**にはあいませんでした。京都には日本中の国宝の 20% 以上が集中しています。以下はほんの一摘みのサンプルです。

　三層の黄金の四阿（あずまや）、金閣寺。1950 年に放火で焼失しましたが、1955 年にそっくりそのまま再建され、その美しさは息を呑むほどです。全体が漆ではりつけた金箔で覆われています。銀閣寺（銀の四阿）は 1482 年に建立されましたが、庭園が有名です。東山で栄えた文化の中心でした。竜安寺は**禅寺**ですが、中庭として、有名な石庭があります。禅の教えをビジュアルに表したものだと言われています。

京都・奈良 [kyoto / nara]
Kyoto & Nara Page 2

Nijo Castle (1603) was originally Tokugawa Ieyasu's Kyoto residence. It is one of Kyoto's 17 World Heritage Sites. Kiyomizu-dera is a temple which has a cypress platform built out over a deep gorge. This sacred dancing stage stands 12 meters above the ground on zelkova pillars. Sanjusangen-do houses 1,001 images of Kannon and disciples of the Buddha. During the Edo period, an archery competition (*toshiya*) was held on the 120-meter-long veranda outside the long hall.

Kyoto is the national center for tea ceremony and flower arrangement. It is also the birthplace of noh, kyogen, kabuki and other traditional performing arts. Its festivals include the Aoi (May), Gion (July) and Jidai (October) festivals. The city is the heart of traditional culture.

(351words)

| Round 1 | Round 2 | Round 3 | Round 4 | Round 5 | Round 6 |
| 月　日 | 月　日 | 月　日 | 月　日 | 月　日 | 月　日 |

　二条城（1603）はもとは徳川家康の京都の居城でした。京都にある17の世界遺産の1つです。清水寺は深い谷の上にせり出しているヒノキの板の舞台が有名です。この聖なる舞踊のためのステージは、地上12メートル、ケヤキの柱に支えられています。三十三間堂には観音菩薩と釈迦の弟子たちの像が1001体あります。江戸時代には、細長いお堂の外にある120メートルの縁側で、弓術の競技である通し矢が行われました。

　京都は日本の茶の湯と生花の中心地です。能、狂言、歌舞伎をはじめとする伝統芸能を生み出したのも京都です。お祭りには葵祭（5月）、祇園祭（7月）、時代祭（10月）などがあります。京都は伝統文化の中心です。

このページに、使ってみたい英語表現や、覚えておきたい英単語などを書き込んでおきましょう

著者紹介

James M. Vardaman　ジェームス・M・バーダマン

1947年、アメリカ、テネシー生まれ。
ハワイ大学アジア研究専攻、修士。
早稲田大学文化構想学部教授。
著書に『毎日の英文法　頭の中に「英語のパターン」をつくる』
『毎日の英単語　日常頻出語の90％をマスターする』
『毎日の英速読　頭の中に「英文読解の回路」をつくる』(以上、小社)、
『アメリカ南部』(講談社)、
『黒人差別とアメリカ公民権運動』(集英社)、など多数ある。

山本 史郎　やまもと・しろう　[日本語訳]

1954年、和歌山県生まれ。
東京大学教養学部教養学科卒業。
東京大学総合文化研究科教授。英文学者。翻訳家。
著書に『名作英文学を読み直す』(講談社)、
『東大の教室で「赤毛のアン」を読む』
『教養英語読本 I・II』(以上、東京大学出版会)、など。
訳書に『ホビット』『完全版 赤毛のアン』(以上、原書房)、
『自分で考えてみる哲学』(東京大学出版会)、など多数ある。

毎日の日本
英語で話す! まるごとJAPAN

2015年3月30日 第1刷発行

著者 James M. Vardaman 山本史郎
装丁・ブックデザイン 寄藤文平+杉山健太郎(文平銀座)
発行者 首藤由之
発行所 朝日新聞出版
　　　　〒104-8011 東京都中央区築地5-3-2
電話　　03-5541-8814(編集)
　　　　03-5540-7793(販売)
印刷所 大日本印刷株式会社
©2015 James M. Vardaman, Shiro Yamamoto
Published in Japan by Asahi Shimbun Publications Inc.
ISBN 978-4-02-331377-4
定価はカバーに表示してあります。
本書掲載の文章・図版の無断複製・転載を禁じます。
落丁・乱丁の場合は弊社業務部(電話 03-5540-7800)へご連絡ください。
送料弊社負担にてお取り替えいたします。